The Go Programming Bible, A Developer's Guide to Building Robust Systems

Advanced Go Concepts and Best Practices for Scalable Software

Booker Blunt

Rafael Sanders

Miguel Farmer

Boozman Richard

Contents

How to Scan a Barcode to Get a Repository

1. **Install a QR/Barcode Scanner** – Ensure you have a barcode or QR code scanner app installed on your smartphone or use a built-in scanner in **GitHub, GitLab, or Bitbucket.**

2. **Open the Scanner** – Launch the scanner app and grant necessary camera permissions.

3. **Scan the Barcode** – Align the barcode within the scanning frame. The scanner will automatically detect and process it.

4. **Follow the Link** – The scanned result will display a **URL to the repository**. Tap the link to open it in your web browser or Git client.

5. **Clone the Repository** – Use **Git clone** with the provided URL to download the repository to your local machine.

Chapter 1: Introduction to Go

1. Introduction

Go is a programming language that emerged from a desire to create a simple, efficient, and reliable tool for building software systems. Developed at a time when modern software was rapidly growing in complexity, Go was designed to address common pain points found in existing languages. In this chapter, we explore the origins of Go, its underlying design philosophy, and how it has found a place in solving real-world challenges.

When you begin learning a new language, understanding its history and core motivations is essential. Go was conceived by a team of experienced engineers who were not satisfied with the difficulties encountered when using older programming languages. They sought to produce a language that would be both easy to read and fast to compile, while also supporting modern computing needs such as concurrency and scalability. As you move forward, you will find that the decisions made during Go's development continue to influence how the language is used in today's software projects.

Key terminology that will recur throughout this chapter includes "concurrency," "goroutines," "channels," and "simplicity." Each of these terms plays a critical role in how Go handles tasks and processes. Concurrency, for example, refers to the ability of a program to perform multiple operations simultaneously. Instead of relying on heavyweight threads, Go uses lightweight processes called goroutines. Channels provide a structured way for these goroutines to communicate with each other, ensuring that data flows smoothly between different parts of an application.

Go's design also emphasizes clarity over cleverness. The language's creators believed that writing code should be straightforward enough that others can easily understand and maintain it. This clarity makes Go an excellent choice for collaborative projects, where readability and reliability are paramount. If you've ever encountered code that is hard to follow due to overcomplicated syntax or ambiguous logic, you'll appreciate Go's approach.

Throughout this chapter, we will explore both the theoretical aspects of Go as well as its practical applications. From understanding how the language handles data types and control structures to setting up your development environment, this introduction aims to build a strong foundation. By the end of this chapter, you will have a clear understanding of why Go was created, how it differs from other languages, and what makes it a compelling option for building robust software systems.

The tone of this chapter is conversational and reflective. It is not just about learning syntax but also about understanding the underlying ideas that guide Go's development. As you progress, think about how these ideas apply to your own work and projects. Whether you are writing small utilities or large-scale enterprise software, the principles behind Go can help guide your design decisions and improve your code's reliability.

2. Core Concepts and Theory

2.1. A Brief History of Go

Go originated at Google in the late 2000s when several engineers decided it was time for a new language that could handle modern hardware and software demands. They were influenced by the desire to create a language that was fast, efficient, and easy to use. This history is reflected in many of the language's features. For instance, Go's simple syntax was developed in response to the perceived complexity of languages like C++ and Java.

The development of Go was also driven by a need for better tools to manage concurrent processes. Many languages at the time either offered inadequate support for concurrency or required cumbersome workarounds. Go addresses this by embedding concurrency as a first-class concept. In practical terms, this means that writing programs that perform multiple tasks simultaneously is both straightforward and efficient.

2.2. Design Philosophy

At its core, Go's design philosophy centers on simplicity and efficiency. The language encourages developers to write clear code that can be easily understood and maintained by others. This approach stands in contrast to languages that reward clever one-liners or overly complex solutions. In Go, the emphasis is on robust, reliable systems that can be built and maintained over time.

Some key design decisions include:

- **Simplicity in Syntax:** Go avoids unnecessary complexity by providing a minimal set of language constructs. For example, there is no inheritance in the traditional object-oriented sense; instead, Go relies on interfaces to define behavior.

- **Built-in Concurrency:** The language introduces goroutines and channels as primary tools for managing concurrent execution. This design allows developers to write efficient, concurrent code with minimal overhead.

- **Fast Compilation:** Go was built to compile quickly, a critical factor when working on large codebases. This speed encourages rapid iteration and testing, which are essential in modern software development.

- **Tooling and Format Enforcement:** The language comes with robust tools such as gofmt to enforce a standard code format. This feature improves readability and reduces errors caused by inconsistent coding styles.

2.3. Real-World Applications of Go

In practice, Go is used in various industries. Its efficiency and concurrency support make it an ideal choice for cloud services, microservices architectures, and large-scale web applications. For instance, many companies in manufacturing, healthcare, and logistics use Go to manage complex systems that require high performance and reliability.

A common scenario where Go shines is in building network servers. With the help of goroutines and channels, a server written in Go can handle thousands of simultaneous connections without becoming overwhelmed. This capability is essential for applications that require low latency and high throughput.

Another area of application is in building command-line tools. Thanks to its fast compilation times and clear syntax, Go is frequently chosen for projects that need to be deployed quickly and run efficiently across different operating systems. Additionally, the language's static typing and straightforward error handling make it easier to identify and fix bugs, which is especially valuable in production environments.

2.4. Setting Learning Goals

Before diving into the hands-on projects and more detailed topics later in the book, it's helpful to define your learning goals. Ask yourself what you hope to achieve by learning Go. Whether you want to improve your career prospects, create personal projects, or simply understand a modern programming language from the ground up, setting clear objectives will help guide your learning process.

Here are some practical steps to define your goals:

- **Reflect on Your Background:** Consider your previous programming experience. If you're new to programming, you might focus on grasping the fundamentals. If you have experience in other languages, you might aim to compare and contrast Go with those languages.

- **Identify Projects That Excite You:** Think about real-world problems you'd like to solve. Perhaps you are interested in

building a web service, creating a command-line tool, or
experimenting with concurrent programming. Knowing what
projects excite you can help tailor your study plan.

- **Plan Your Time:** Learning a new language takes time and effort.
  Decide how much time you can dedicate each week to studying
  and practicing. Setting aside regular intervals for learning and
  coding can significantly boost your progress.

- **Leverage Community Resources:** There is a vibrant community
  around Go. Joining forums, reading blogs, and contributing to
  open-source projects can provide additional support and
  inspiration. This chapter and the subsequent ones are designed to
  be part of a larger journey. Engage actively with available
  resources, ask questions, and share your own experiences as you
  build proficiency in Go.

2.5. Go as a Problem-Solving Tool

One of the most appealing aspects of Go is its focus on solving real
problems. From backend development to distributed systems, Go
provides a solid foundation for tackling modern computing challenges.
The language's straightforward error handling, combined with its native
support for concurrency, means that developers can create applications
that are both efficient and robust.

Imagine you're tasked with creating a service that processes data in real-
time. Go's lightweight goroutines allow you to perform multiple data
processing tasks concurrently. At the same time, channels help coordinate

these tasks without the need for complex synchronization mechanisms. These features collectively reduce the chances of bugs that can occur in a multi-threaded environment, making your solutions more reliable.

The combination of simplicity, performance, and strong support for concurrency positions Go as a competitive option for solving problems that demand high reliability. Whether you're automating tasks or building systems that operate at scale, Go's design principles help streamline the development process.

---

3. Tools and Setup

3.1. Installing Go

Before writing your first line of code, you need to set up your development environment. The installation process for Go is straightforward across major operating systems—Windows, macOS, and Linux. You can download the latest stable release from the official Go website.

Step-by-Step Installation:

1. **Visit the Official Site:** Navigate to golang.org/dl.

2. **Select the Installer:** Choose the appropriate installer for your operating system.

3. **Run the Installer:** Follow the on-screen instructions to complete the installation.

4. **Verify the Installation:** Open a terminal or command prompt and type:

```
bash
```

```
go version
```

You should see output similar to go version go1.xx.x confirming that Go is installed.

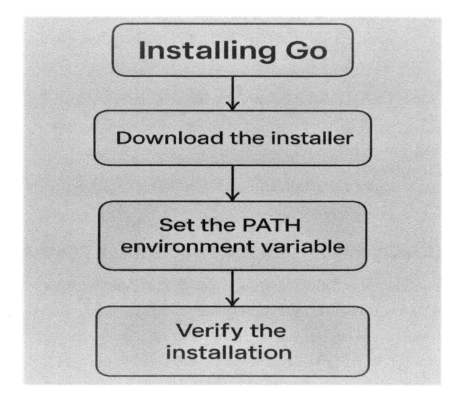

3.2. Setting Up Your IDE

While you can write Go code in any text editor, using an Integrated Development Environment (IDE) can simplify the process. Popular choices include Visual Studio Code with the Go extension, GoLand, and

Sublime Text. These environments offer features like syntax highlighting, code completion, and integrated debugging tools.

Setting Up Visual Studio Code for Go:

1. **Install Visual Studio Code:** Download and install VS Code from its official website.

2. **Install the Go Extension:** Launch VS Code, go to the Extensions panel, and search for "Go." Install the extension provided by the Go team.

3. **Configure the Environment:** The extension may prompt you to install additional tools (e.g., gopls for language features). Follow these instructions to ensure a smooth setup.

4. **Create a New Project:** Open a new folder and create a file named main.go to start coding.

3.3. Command-Line Tools and Version Control

In addition to an IDE, you will benefit from familiarity with command-line tools. The Go toolchain includes commands for building, testing, and managing dependencies. Additionally, using version control systems like Git will help manage your codebase and collaborate with others.

Essential Commands:

- **Building a Project:**

```bash
go build main.go
```

This command compiles your Go program into an executable.

- **Running Tests:**

```bash
go test ./...
```
This command runs all tests in your project directories.

- **Formatting Code:**

```bash
go fmt ./...
```
Enforce a consistent code style across your files.

3.4. Recommended Resources

For additional support during setup, consider these resources:

- **Official Documentation:** The Go documentation is a comprehensive source of truth for language features and best practices.

- **Community Forums:** Sites like the Golang subreddit and various Go forums provide practical advice from fellow developers.

- **Video Tutorials:** Numerous free tutorials are available on platforms like YouTube that visually guide you through the installation and configuration process.

By completing these setup steps, you create a solid foundation for building projects with Go. You now have the tools to write, test, and debug your code efficiently.

4. Hands-on Examples & Projects

4.1. Your First Go Program

Let's start with a simple program that prints a greeting message. This "Hello, World!" example is a classic way to confirm that your environment is set up correctly.

Example:

```go
package main

import "fmt"

// main is the entry point of the program.
func main() {
    fmt.Println("Hello, Go!")
}
```

Explanation:

This code defines a package named main and imports the fmt package for formatted I/O operations. The main function is where execution begins, and fmt.Println outputs a message to the console.

4.2. A Basic Calculator

To illustrate basic syntax and data handling, we will create a calculator that performs arithmetic operations. This project demonstrates reading input, processing calculations, and outputting results.

Code Example:

```go
go

package main

import (
    "fmt"
    "os"
    "strconv"
)

// simpleCalculator performs addition, subtraction,
multiplication, and division.
func simpleCalculator(a, b float64, operator string)
float64 {
    switch operator {
    case "+":
        return a + b
    case "-":
        return a - b
    case "*":
        return a * b
    case "/":
        if b != 0 {
            return a / b
        }
        fmt.Println("Division by zero error!")
        os.Exit(1)
    default:
        fmt.Println("Unsupported operator!")
        os.Exit(1)
    }
    return 0
}

func main() {
    var op string
    var num1Str, num2Str string

    fmt.Print("Enter first number: ")
    fmt.Scanln(&num1Str)
    fmt.Print("Enter operator (+, -, *, /): ")
    fmt.Scanln(&op)
    fmt.Print("Enter second number: ")
    fmt.Scanln(&num2Str)
```

```
    num1, err1 := strconv.ParseFloat(num1Str, 64)
    num2, err2 := strconv.ParseFloat(num2Str, 64)
    if err1 != nil || err2 != nil {
        fmt.Println("Invalid input! Please enter
numeric values.")
        return
    }

    result := simpleCalculator(num1, num2, op)
    fmt.Printf("Result: %.2f\n", result)
}
```

Explanation:

This program uses the fmt, os, and strconv packages. It reads user input for two numbers and an operator, converts the string inputs to floating-point numbers, performs the appropriate calculation based on the operator, and prints the result. The use of a switch statement in the simpleCalculator function illustrates Go's clean control structures.

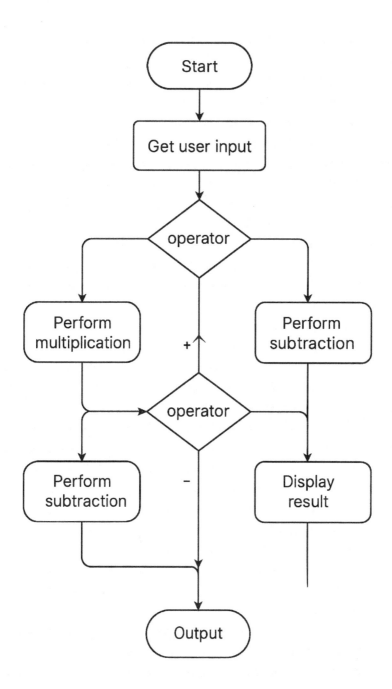

4.3. Building a Contact Manager

Now, let's build a more engaging project—a simple contact manager. This project demonstrates working with data structures, file I/O, and basic CRUD (create, read, update, delete) operations.

Code Example:

```go
package main

import (
    "bufio"
    "encoding/json"
    "fmt"
    "os"
    "strings"
)

// Contact represents a contact entry.
type Contact struct {
    Name  string `json:"name"`
    Phone string `json:"phone"`
}

// loadContacts reads contacts from a JSON file.
func loadContacts(filename string) ([]Contact, error) {
    file, err := os.Open(filename)
    if err != nil {
        return nil, err
    }
    defer file.Close()

    var contacts []Contact
    decoder := json.NewDecoder(file)
    if err := decoder.Decode(&contacts); err != nil {
        return nil, err
    }
    return contacts, nil
```

```go
}

// saveContacts writes contacts to a JSON file.
func saveContacts(filename string, contacts
[]Contact) error {
    file, err := os.Create(filename)
    if err != nil {
        return err
    }
    defer file.Close()

    encoder := json.NewEncoder(file)
    return encoder.Encode(contacts)
}

func main() {
    const filename = "contacts.json"
    contacts, err := loadContacts(filename)
    if err != nil {
        fmt.Println("No existing contacts found.
Starting fresh.")
        contacts = []Contact{}
    }

    reader := bufio.NewReader(os.Stdin)
    for {
        fmt.Println("\nContact Manager Options:")
        fmt.Println("1. List Contacts")
        fmt.Println("2. Add Contact")
        fmt.Println("3. Update Contact")
        fmt.Println("4. Delete Contact")
        fmt.Println("5. Exit")
        fmt.Print("Select an option: ")
        choice, _ := reader.ReadString('\n')
        choice = strings.TrimSpace(choice)

        switch choice {
        case "1":
            fmt.Println("\nCurrent Contacts:")
            for _, c := range contacts {
                fmt.Printf("Name: %s, Phone: %s\n",
c.Name, c.Phone)
            }
        case "2":
```

```
        fmt.Print("Enter name: ")
        name, _ := reader.ReadString('\n')
        fmt.Print("Enter phone: ")
        phone, _ := reader.ReadString('\n')
        contacts = append(contacts,
Contact{strings.TrimSpace(name),
strings.TrimSpace(phone)})
        fmt.Println("Contact added.")
    case "3":
        fmt.Print("Enter name of contact to
update: ")
        name, _ := reader.ReadString('\n')
        name = strings.TrimSpace(name)
        updated := false
        for i, c := range contacts {
            if c.Name == name {
                fmt.Print("Enter new phone: ")
                newPhone, _ :=
reader.ReadString('\n')
                contacts[i].Phone =
strings.TrimSpace(newPhone)
                fmt.Println("Contact updated.")
                updated = true
                break
            }
        }
        if !updated {
            fmt.Println("Contact not found.")
        }
    case "4":
        fmt.Print("Enter name of contact to
delete: ")
        name, _ := reader.ReadString('\n')
        name = strings.TrimSpace(name)
        newContacts := []Contact{}
        for _, c := range contacts {
            if c.Name != name {
                newContacts = append(newContacts,
c)
            }
        }
        contacts = newContacts
        fmt.Println("Contact deleted if it
existed.")
```

```
        case "5":
            if err := saveContacts(filename,
contacts); err != nil {
                fmt.Println("Error saving contacts:",
err)
            }
            fmt.Println("Exiting Contact Manager.")
            return
        default:
            fmt.Println("Invalid option. Please try
again.")
        }
    }
}
```

Explanation:

This contact manager uses JSON for data storage. It loads existing contacts from a file, allows the user to perform CRUD operations through a simple text interface, and saves changes back to the file. The code demonstrates the use of structures, slices, file operations, and JSON encoding/decoding in Go.

4.4. A Concurrent Data Processor

Go's support for concurrency is one of its most powerful features. In this example, we create a concurrent data processor that simulates processing multiple data streams simultaneously using goroutines and channels.

Code Example:

```go
go

package main

import (
    "fmt"
    "math/rand"
    "time"
)
```

```go
// processData simulates processing data and sends
the result on a channel.
func processData(id int, results chan<- string) {
    delay := rand.Intn(1000)
    time.Sleep(time.Millisecond *
time.Duration(delay))
    results <- fmt.Sprintf("Goroutine %d finished
processing in %d ms", id, delay)
}

func main() {
    rand.Seed(time.Now().UnixNano())
    results := make(chan string, 5)
    numWorkers := 5

    // Start multiple goroutines to process data
concurrently.
    for i := 1; i <= numWorkers; i++ {
        go processData(i, results)
    }

    // Collect and display results.
    for i := 0; i < numWorkers; i++ {
        fmt.Println(<-results)
    }
}
```

Explanation:

This snippet illustrates how to use goroutines to process tasks concurrently. Each goroutine simulates a data processing task by sleeping for a random amount of time before sending a result through a channel. The main function waits for all goroutines to complete by reading from the channel.

4.5. Putting It All Together

In this section, you will integrate the lessons learned so far by developing a mini-project that combines user input, data processing, and concurrent operations. The project simulates a system that receives requests, processes them concurrently, and then logs the results.

Project Outline:

- **Objective:** Create a simulated request handler that accepts user input, spawns goroutines for processing, and outputs the results.

- **Steps:**

  1. Read user input for the number of simulated requests.

  2. Spawn a goroutine for each request.

  3. Use channels to collect results.

  4. Print a summary of all processed requests.

Code Example:

```go
package main

import (
    "bufio"
    "fmt"
    "math/rand"
    "os"
    "strconv"
    "strings"
    "time"
)

// simulateRequest mimics processing a request.
func simulateRequest(id int, results chan<- string) {
    delay := rand.Intn(1500)
    time.Sleep(time.Millisecond *
time.Duration(delay))
```

```go
    results <- fmt.Sprintf("Request %d processed in
%d ms", id, delay)
}

func main() {
    rand.Seed(time.Now().UnixNano())
    reader := bufio.NewReader(os.Stdin)

    fmt.Print("Enter number of requests to simulate:
")
    input, _ := reader.ReadString('\n')
    input = strings.TrimSpace(input)
    numRequests, err := strconv.Atoi(input)
    if err != nil {
        fmt.Println("Invalid input. Please enter an
integer.")
        return
    }

    results := make(chan string, numRequests)

    // Spawn a goroutine for each request.
    for i := 1; i <= numRequests; i++ {
        go simulateRequest(i, results)
    }

    // Collect results.
    for i := 0; i < numRequests; i++ {
        fmt.Println(<-results)
    }
    fmt.Println("All requests processed
successfully.")
}
```

Explanation:

This program encapsulates multiple core Go concepts—user input, goroutines for concurrency, and channels for synchronization. By combining these ideas, you create a robust simulation that models how concurrent systems handle multiple tasks. This mini-project illustrates how Go can be used in real-world scenarios where multiple processes must operate in parallel without complex synchronization code.

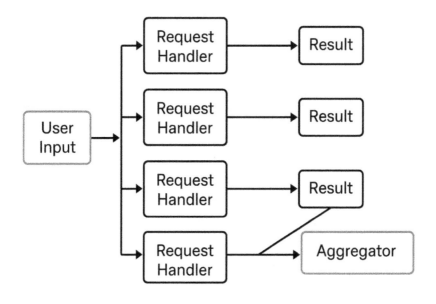

5 . Conclusion & Next Steps

This chapter has provided a solid introduction to Go by covering its history, design principles, and real-world applications. We began with the origins and philosophy behind Go, moved through the core concepts that define the language, and set up a working environment complete with tools and best practices. In the hands-on section, you tackled several projects—from simple programs like "Hello, World!" to more complex projects like a concurrent data processor and a contact manager. Along the way, you learned strategies for optimizing performance and troubleshooting common issues.

Looking ahead, the next chapters will build on these foundations. You will explore more advanced topics such as in-depth concurrency patterns, robust testing methodologies, and advanced error handling techniques. As you continue, keep experimenting with the projects introduced here and consider how these techniques can be applied to your own work. The key is to remain curious, ask questions, and be willing to iterate on your solutions.

For further reading, consider visiting the official Go documentation, joining community forums, and exploring additional tutorials. These resources can provide more detailed explanations and help you stay updated with the latest improvements in Go. By embracing the ideas and practices discussed in this chapter, you are well on your way to building robust, efficient systems using Go.

Thank you for investing time in learning these fundamentals. As you progress, remember that every error encountered and every problem solved adds to your expertise. Your next steps might involve deeper dives into advanced topics, experimenting with larger projects, or even contributing to open-source Go projects. Keep pushing the boundaries of what you can create with this versatile language.

Happy coding, and may your code be clear, efficient, and resilient!

Chapter 2: Setting Up Your Environment

1. Introduction

Programming is as much about having the right tools as it is about writing code. In this chapter, we focus on preparing your workspace for Go development. Whether you are a beginner stepping into coding for the first time, a professional looking to refine your workflow, or a hobbyist curious about exploring a new language, setting up a proper environment is a key step toward success.

The significance of an optimized development environment cannot be overstated. A well-configured setup not only accelerates your coding process but also minimizes errors and supports better code maintenance. Here, you will learn the terminology that underpins the process—terms like "compiler," "runtime," "IDE" (Integrated Development Environment), and "text editor." We explain what these mean in plain language and why each one matters when working with Go.

Our journey begins with installing the Go language itself. You will learn how to download the official release, execute the installer, and verify that your installation was successful. Then, we'll explore different tools that support Go development, including popular IDEs and text editors. You'll discover that while some developers swear by fully featured IDEs, others prefer lighter-weight editors; both approaches have merits depending on your project's scale and your personal style.

Throughout this chapter, the tone is professional and encouraging. The steps are laid out clearly to help you establish a reliable foundation from which to write and test Go code. By the end of this chapter, you should feel confident that your system is ready to support Go programming, whether you are building small command-line utilities or large-scale applications.

Imagine sitting at your desk with a clear screen, a terminal window open, and your favorite code editor ready to accept new ideas. This chapter will show you how to transform that vision into reality. You'll learn to configure everything from your operating system's environment variables to the language-specific tools that come with Go. Along the way, you'll see code examples that demonstrate how to run a simple Go program and verify that everything works as expected.

By investing time into this setup process, you save yourself the headaches of debugging environment issues later on. A stable environment is a sign of a healthy development cycle—it ensures that the focus remains on solving real problems with code rather than wrestling with configuration errors.

Let's now move into the heart of the matter: understanding the core concepts behind the tools and techniques needed for setting up Go. In the next section, we'll explore the underlying theory that makes these tools indispensable for efficient programming.

2. Core Concepts and Theory

Before we dive into installation and configuration, it's useful to explore the ideas that drive a robust development environment. At its foundation, a development environment is a combination of software, settings, and processes designed to make coding, testing, and deploying applications smoother.

2.1. What Is a Development Environment?

A development environment comprises several components:

- **Compiler and Runtime:** For Go, the compiler translates your source code into an executable binary. The runtime supports features such as garbage collection and concurrent execution.

- **Text Editor/IDE:** The interface where you write code. Editors can range from basic (like Vim or Nano) to advanced IDEs (like Visual Studio Code or GoLand) that offer features like debugging, syntax highlighting, and version control integration.

- **Command-Line Interface (CLI):** Many programming tasks, such as building code, running tests, and managing packages, are executed via the terminal. Familiarity with command-line operations is essential.

- **Version Control:** Tools like Git manage changes to your code, enabling collaboration and ensuring you can track the evolution of your projects.

- **Build Tools:** These automate repetitive tasks such as code compilation, testing, and packaging.

Understanding these components is key. For example, when you run a command like go build, the Go compiler is invoked, and your source code is processed to produce an executable file. This process is supported by a series of environment variables that control where Go looks for packages, how it caches compiled files, and more.

2.2. The Role of IDEs and Text Editors

An Integrated Development Environment (IDE) is more than just a text editor. It combines several functionalities into one cohesive interface. Popular IDEs like Visual Studio Code and GoLand provide:

- **Syntax Highlighting:** Colors different parts of your code (such as keywords, strings, and comments) to enhance readability.

- **IntelliSense/Auto-Completion:** Offers code suggestions as you type, reducing errors and speeding up coding.

- **Debugging Tools:** Allow you to set breakpoints, step through code, and inspect variable values during execution.

- **Integrated Terminal:** Enables you to run CLI commands without leaving the editor.

On the other hand, lightweight text editors such as Sublime Text or Vim are prized for their speed and flexibility. They often require manual configuration and plugins to support language-specific features, but many developers appreciate the minimalism and speed they offer.

2.3. Command-Line Proficiency

Even if you prefer an IDE, command-line skills remain crucial. Most Go operations are performed in a terminal. Commands such as go run, go test, and go fmt are staples in the Go ecosystem. The command line gives you direct control over the build process and allows for scripting repetitive tasks.

2.4. Environment Variables and Path Settings

When installing Go, you will encounter environment variables like GOROOT and GOPATH.

- **GOROOT:** Points to the location where Go is installed.

- **GOPATH:** Represents your workspace where Go projects and packages reside.

Configuring these correctly ensures that your system can locate the Go tools and libraries. Misconfigured paths can lead to errors that are sometimes difficult to diagnose.

2.5. Real-World Implications

Imagine a scenario where you're part of a team developing a web service in Go. A misconfigured development environment might lead to "works on my machine" issues, where code runs on one computer but fails on another. By standardizing the environment with clear instructions and automation, teams can collaborate more effectively and reduce troubleshooting time.

The theory behind these tools is simple yet powerful: they are designed to remove friction from the development process. A well-set-up environment allows you to concentrate on writing code and solving problems rather than dealing with setup issues. This concept is echoed across many programming languages but finds a particularly smooth implementation in Go due to its emphasis on simplicity and efficiency.

As you become familiar with these core concepts, you'll appreciate how each piece—from the compiler to the text editor—fits into the larger picture of software development. In the next section, we will translate these concepts into actionable steps as we walk through the tools and setup process for Go.

3. Tools and Setup

Before you write a single line of Go code, you must ensure that your system is properly configured. This section outlines the tools you need and provides step-by-step instructions for setting up your environment.

3.1. Required Tools and Platforms

The primary tools for Go development include:

- **Go Language:** Downloadable from the official Go website.

- **Command-Line Interface (CLI):** Built into your operating system (e.g., Terminal on macOS/Linux or Command Prompt/PowerShell on Windows).

- **IDE/Text Editor:** Popular choices include Visual Studio Code, GoLand, Sublime Text, and Vim.

- **Version Control System:** Git is the most common choice, available from git-scm.com.

3.2. Installing Go

Follow these steps to install Go on your system:

1. **Download the Installer:**

   Visit golang.org/dl and select the installer for your operating system.

   Visual Aid: Imagine a screenshot showing the download page with options for Windows, macOS, and Linux.

2. **Run the Installer:**

   Execute the downloaded installer and follow the on-screen instructions. Accept the default settings unless you have specific needs.

3. **Verify the Installation:**

   Open your terminal or command prompt and type:

```bash
go version
```

You should see output similar to go version go1.XX.X confirming the installation.

4. **Set Environment Variables (if necessary):**

   On some systems, you may need to set GOROOT (the Go

installation directory) and GOPATH (your workspace directory). For example, on Unix-like systems, add the following lines to your shell configuration file (e.g., .bashrc or .zshrc):

```bash
export GOROOT=/usr/local/go
export GOPATH=$HOME/go
export PATH=$PATH:$GOROOT/bin:$GOPATH/bin
```

```
user@hostname:~$ vim ~/.bashrc

~

~   # Go Environment Variables
~   export GOROOT=/usr/local/go
~   export GOPATH=$HOME/go
~   export PATH=$PATH:$GOROOT/bin:$GOPATH/bin
~
~
~
~
    "~/.bashrc" [New File]
```

3.3. Setting Up an IDE or Text Editor

While you can code in any editor, using an IDE or a feature-rich text editor can significantly improve your workflow. Below, we outline how to set up Visual Studio Code (VS Code), a popular choice among Go developers:

1. **Install VS Code:**

   Download VS Code from code.visualstudio.com and follow the installation instructions for your operating system.

2. **Install the Go Extension:**

   Launch VS Code, navigate to the Extensions pane (using the sidebar or pressing Ctrl+Shift+X), and search for "Go". Install the extension maintained by the Go team.

   Visual Aid: A screenshot showing the VS Code extensions page with the Go extension highlighted.

3. **Configure Additional Tools:**

   The Go extension may prompt you to install supplementary tools like gopls (for language features) and dlv (for debugging). Follow the instructions provided in VS Code to complete these installations.

4. **Create a New Go Project:**

   Open a folder where you want your project to reside. Create a new file named main.go and write a simple Go program. We will cover running this program in the next section.

3.4. Version Control Setup

Installing Git is highly recommended. Visit git-scm.com to download and install Git on your machine. Once installed, configure your user details by running:

```bash
git config --global user.name "Your Name"
```

```
git config --global user.email
"youremail@example.com"
```
This configuration ensures that your commits are properly attributed and is an essential step for collaborating on projects.

By following these steps, you will create a stable and efficient development environment that supports your Go programming endeavors. In the next major section, we will put these tools to work with hands-on examples and projects.

4. Hands-on Examples & Projects

With your environment set up, it's time to roll up your sleeves and start coding. This section is dedicated to practical examples that help you understand how to write, run, and debug your first Go programs.

4.1. Writing and Running Your First Go Program

Let's begin with the classic "Hello, World!" program. This simple example verifies that your installation works correctly.

Hello, World! Example:

```go
go

package main

import "fmt"

// main is the entry point of the program.
func main() {
    fmt.Println("Hello, World!")
}
```

Explanation:

This program declares a package named main and imports the fmt package to perform formatted I/O. The main function serves as the entry point, and the program outputs "Hello, World!" to the console.

Step-by-Step Execution:

1. **Create the File:**
   Open your IDE or text editor, create a new file named main.go, and paste the code above.

2. **Save and Run:**
   Open your terminal, navigate to the folder containing main.go, and run:

```bash
```

```
go run main.go
```
3. **Observe the Output:**
   The terminal should display:

```
Hello, World!
```

4.2. Building a Simple Command-Line Application

Now, let's build a basic command-line calculator that accepts two numbers and an operator. This project introduces you to reading user input, error handling, and basic arithmetic operations.

Calculator Example:

```go
go

package main

import (
    "bufio"
    "fmt"
    "os"
    "strconv"
    "strings"
)

// simpleCalculator performs arithmetic operations
based on the operator.
func simpleCalculator(a, b float64, operator string)
float64 {
    switch operator {
    case "+":
        return a + b
    case "-":
        return a - b
    case "*":
        return a * b
    case "/":
        if b != 0 {
            return a / b
        }
        fmt.Println("Error: Division by zero.")
        os.Exit(1)
    default:
        fmt.Println("Error: Unsupported operator.")
        os.Exit(1)
    }
    return 0
}

func main() {
    reader := bufio.NewReader(os.Stdin)

    fmt.Print("Enter first number: ")
    num1Str, _ := reader.ReadString('\n')
    num1Str = strings.TrimSpace(num1Str)
    num1, err := strconv.ParseFloat(num1Str, 64)
    if err != nil {
```

```
        fmt.Println("Invalid input for first
number.")
        return
    }

    fmt.Print("Enter operator (+, -, *, /): ")
    operator, _ := reader.ReadString('\n')
    operator = strings.TrimSpace(operator)

    fmt.Print("Enter second number: ")
    num2Str, _ := reader.ReadString('\n')
    num2Str = strings.TrimSpace(num2Str)
    num2, err := strconv.ParseFloat(num2Str, 64)
    if err != nil {
        fmt.Println("Invalid input for second
number.")
        return
    }

    result := simpleCalculator(num1, num2, operator)
    fmt.Printf("Result: %.2f\n", result)
}
```

Explanation:

This code snippet illustrates how to read user input using a buffered reader, convert string inputs to floating-point numbers, and apply a simple calculator function. The switch statement is used to decide which arithmetic operation to perform.

```
flowchart TD
    A[Start] --> B[Input: First Number]
    A --> C[Input: Operator]
    A --> D[Input: Second Number]
    B --> E[Calculation Process]
    C --> E
    D --> E
    E --> F[Final Output]
```

4.3. Creating a Project Structure

As your projects grow, it's essential to maintain a structured layout. In Go, a common approach is to separate code into packages. Let's create a simple project structure:

- **Project Folder:** go-project

  o main.go

  o calculator/

    ▪ calculator.go

  o README.md

File: calculator/calculator.go

```go
package calculator

import "fmt"

// Calculate performs arithmetic based on the
provided operator.
func Calculate(a, b float64, operator string)
(float64, error) {
    switch operator {
    case "+":
        return a + b, nil
    case "-":
        return a - b, nil
    case "*":
        return a * b, nil
    case "/":
        if b != 0 {
```

```go
        return a / b, nil
    }
    return 0, fmt.Errorf("division by zero")
default:
    return 0, fmt.Errorf("unsupported operator")
    }
}
```

File: main.go

```go
go

package main

import (
    "bufio"
    "fmt"
    "go-project/calculator"
    "os"
    "strconv"
    "strings"
)

func main() {
    reader := bufio.NewReader(os.Stdin)
    fmt.Print("Enter first number: ")
    num1Str, _ := reader.ReadString('\n')
    num1, err :=
strconv.ParseFloat(strings.TrimSpace(num1Str), 64)
    if err != nil {
        fmt.Println("Invalid input for first
number.")
        return
    }

    fmt.Print("Enter operator (+, -, *, /): ")
    operator, _ := reader.ReadString('\n')
    operator = strings.TrimSpace(operator)

    fmt.Print("Enter second number: ")
    num2Str, _ := reader.ReadString('\n')
    num2, err :=
strconv.ParseFloat(strings.TrimSpace(num2Str), 64)
    if err != nil {
```

```
        fmt.Println("Invalid input for second
number.")
        return
    }

    result, err := calculator.Calculate(num1, num2,
operator)
    if err != nil {
        fmt.Println("Error:", err)
        return
    }
    fmt.Printf("Result: %.2f\n", result)
}
```

Explanation:

Here, the code is modularized. The calculation logic is moved into its own package, making it easier to maintain and test. The main program imports the calculator package and handles user input.

4.4. Running and Testing Your Projects

After writing your code, the next step is to run and test your application. Use the following commands in your terminal:

- **Run the Application:**

```bash

go run main.go
```
- **Build the Application:**

```bash

go build
```
- **Execute the Binary:**

```bash

./go-project  # or go-project.exe on Windows
```

Testing is also vital. Create tests to validate your functions. For instance, in the calculator package, you might add a file named calculator_test.go:

File: calculator/calculator_test.go

```go
package calculator

import "testing"

func TestCalculate(t *testing.T) {
    tests := []struct {
        a, b       float64
        operator string
        expected float64
        err        bool
    }{
        {5, 3, "+", 8, false},
        {5, 3, "-", 2, false},
        {5, 3, "*", 15, false},
        {6, 3, "/", 2, false},
        {6, 0, "/", 0, true},
        {5, 3, "%", 0, true},
    }
    for _, tt := range tests {
        result, err := Calculate(tt.a, tt.b,
tt.operator)
        if (err != nil) != tt.err {
            t.Errorf("Calculate(%f, %f, %s) error =
%v, expected error? %v", tt.a, tt.b, tt.operator,
err, tt.err)
            continue
        }
        if !tt.err && result != tt.expected {
            t.Errorf("Calculate(%f, %f, %s) = %f,
expected %f", tt.a, tt.b, tt.operator, result,
tt.expected)
        }
    }
}
```

Explanation:

This test file runs a series of cases to ensure that the Calculate function behaves as expected. Running tests with:

```bash
```

```
go test ./calculator
```
will verify the functionality of your code.

4.5. A Mini-Project: Building a Simple To-Do List Application

For a more comprehensive exercise, let's build a simple command-line to-do list manager. This project will integrate user input, file I/O, and basic CRUD operations.

Project Outline:

- **Features:**

  o   Add a new task

  o   List all tasks

  o   Mark tasks as complete

  o   Delete tasks

- **Data Storage:**
  Use a JSON file to store the tasks persistently.

File: todo/todo.go

```go
```

```go
package todo

import (
    "encoding/json"
    "fmt"
    "io/ioutil"
    "os"
)

// Task represents a single to-do item.
type Task struct {
    ID      int    `json:"id"`
    Title   string `json:"title"`
    Done    bool   `json:"done"`
}

// LoadTasks loads tasks from a JSON file.
func LoadTasks(filename string) ([]Task, error) {
    if _, err := os.Stat(filename);
os.IsNotExist(err) {
        return []Task{}, nil
    }
    data, err := ioutil.ReadFile(filename)
    if err != nil {
        return nil, err
    }
    var tasks []Task
    if err := json.Unmarshal(data, &tasks); err !=
nil {
        return nil, err
    }
    return tasks, nil
}

// SaveTasks saves tasks to a JSON file.
func SaveTasks(filename string, tasks []Task) error {
    data, err := json.MarshalIndent(tasks, "", "  ")
    if err != nil {
        return err
    }
    return ioutil.WriteFile(filename, data, 0644)
}

// AddTask adds a new task to the list.
```

```go
func AddTask(tasks []Task, title string) ([]Task,
error) {
    id := 1
    if len(tasks) > 0 {
        id = tasks[len(tasks)-1].ID + 1
    }
    newTask := Task{ID: id, Title: title, Done:
false}
    tasks = append(tasks, newTask)
    return tasks, nil
}

// MarkDone marks a task as complete.
func MarkDone(tasks []Task, id int) ([]Task, error) {
    for i, task := range tasks {
        if task.ID == id {
            tasks[i].Done = true
            return tasks, nil
        }
    }
    return tasks, fmt.Errorf("task with id %d not
found", id)
}

// DeleteTask removes a task by ID.
func DeleteTask(tasks []Task, id int) ([]Task, error)
{
    for i, task := range tasks {
        if task.ID == id {
            tasks = append(tasks[:i], tasks[i+1:]...)
            return tasks, nil
        }
    }
    return tasks, fmt.Errorf("task with id %d not
found", id)
}
```

File: main.go

```go
go

package main

import (
```

```go
    "bufio"
    "fmt"
    "go-project/todo"
    "os"
    "strconv"
    "strings"
)

const filename = "tasks.json"

func main() {
    tasks, err := todo.LoadTasks(filename)
    if err != nil {
        fmt.Println("Error loading tasks:", err)
        return
    }
    reader := bufio.NewReader(os.Stdin)

    for {
        fmt.Println("\nTo-Do List Manager")
        fmt.Println("1. List Tasks")
        fmt.Println("2. Add Task")
        fmt.Println("3. Mark Task as Done")
        fmt.Println("4. Delete Task")
        fmt.Println("5. Exit")
        fmt.Print("Select an option: ")
        option, _ := reader.ReadString('\n')
        option = strings.TrimSpace(option)

        switch option {
        case "1":
            if len(tasks) == 0 {
                fmt.Println("No tasks available.")
            } else {
                fmt.Println("Tasks:")
                for _, task := range tasks {
                    status := "Pending"
                    if task.Done {
                        status = "Done"
                    }
                    fmt.Printf("[%d] %s - %s\n",
task.ID, task.Title, status)
                }
            }
```

```go
    case "2":
        fmt.Print("Enter task title: ")
        title, _ := reader.ReadString('\n')
        title = strings.TrimSpace(title)
        tasks, err = todo.AddTask(tasks, title)
        if err != nil {
            fmt.Println("Error adding task:",
err)
        } else {
            fmt.Println("Task added.")
        }
    case "3":
        fmt.Print("Enter task ID to mark as done:
")
        idStr, _ := reader.ReadString('\n')
        id, err :=
strconv.Atoi(strings.TrimSpace(idStr))
        if err != nil {
            fmt.Println("Invalid ID.")
            continue
        }
        tasks, err = todo.MarkDone(tasks, id)
        if err != nil {
            fmt.Println("Error:", err)
        } else {
            fmt.Println("Task marked as done.")
        }
    case "4":
        fmt.Print("Enter task ID to delete: ")
        idStr, _ := reader.ReadString('\n')
        id, err :=
strconv.Atoi(strings.TrimSpace(idStr))
        if err != nil {
            fmt.Println("Invalid ID.")
            continue
        }
        tasks, err = todo.DeleteTask(tasks, id)
        if err != nil {
            fmt.Println("Error:", err)
        } else {
            fmt.Println("Task deleted.")
        }
    case "5":
```

```
        if err := todo.SaveTasks(filename,
tasks); err != nil {
            fmt.Println("Error saving tasks:",
err)
        } else {
            fmt.Println("Tasks saved. Goodbye!")
        }
        return
    default:
        fmt.Println("Invalid option, please try
again.")
    }
  }
}
```

Explanation:

This to-do list application demonstrates file I/O, JSON data handling, and basic CRUD operations. The project is structured into its own package (todo) and a main file that provides the user interface. Users can list, add, mark, and delete tasks, with persistent storage in a JSON file.

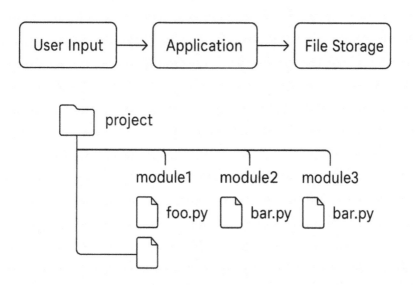

4.6. Summary of Hands-on Section

By now, you have written and run your first Go programs—from the classic "Hello, World!" to more complex command-line applications such as a calculator and a to-do list manager. You've seen how to modularize your code into packages, run tests to verify functionality, and use version control to manage your code.

This hands-on section reinforces the idea that a well-set-up environment isn't just about installing software; it's about creating a productive workflow that lets you focus on solving problems through code. With each project, you have gained familiarity with command-line tools, file I/O, JSON processing, and modular code organization.

5 . Conclusion & Next Steps

In this chapter, you've transformed your computer into a ready-to-code environment for Go. You learned how to install Go, configure essential environment variables, set up popular IDEs like Visual Studio Code, and integrate version control. The hands-on projects—from your first "Hello, World!" program to a multi-featured to-do list manager—demonstrated that a robust setup not only saves time but also empowers you to focus on solving problems with code.

The techniques and tools discussed here are designed to serve as a springboard for your future projects. As you advance, you may choose to explore more sophisticated development workflows or customize your setup to better suit your style. Regularly updating your tools and staying engaged with the community will ensure that your environment remains secure, efficient, and in line with the latest best practices.

Your next steps include:

- **Experimentation:** Modify the example projects, add new features, and try out different IDE configurations.

- **Further Learning:** Explore additional resources, such as Go's official blog and community tutorials, to deepen your understanding.

- **Collaboration:** Begin using version control extensively by contributing to open-source projects or collaborating with other developers.

Reflect on what you've learned in this chapter. A well-configured environment is the foundation of effective programming, and by investing in it now, you set yourself up for success in all future projects. Remember, every error resolved and every configuration refined brings you closer to mastering not just Go, but the art of software development.

As you move forward, consider revisiting your setup periodically. Technology evolves, and with it, so do the tools and best practices. Stay curious, keep learning, and adapt your environment to suit your growing skills. Whether you are writing a small utility or a large-scale application, the skills and practices you've developed here will serve you well throughout your programming career.

Thank you for working through this chapter. With your environment set up and your first projects under your belt, you are now ready to explore more advanced topics and real-world applications in Go. Embrace the process of continuous improvement—each challenge you overcome in setting up or optimizing your tools is a step toward becoming a more proficient developer.

Happy coding, and may your environment always be stable, your code clear, and your debugging sessions brief!

Chapter 3: Basic Syntax and Data Types

1. Introduction

Programming languages serve as the bridge between human ideas and machine instructions. In this chapter, we take a close look at Go's basic syntax and data types. Whether you are a newcomer who has never written a line of code before, a professional developer eager to understand Go's design choices, or a hobbyist interested in exploring another language, the basics covered here are your first step toward mastering Go.

At its core, every programming language has its own way of expressing ideas. Go was created to be straightforward and easy to understand. Its syntax avoids unnecessary complications, enabling you to write code that is clean and maintainable. Here, we will introduce you to the language's keywords, how to work with variables and constants, and the fundamental data types that form the building blocks of any Go program.

You might wonder why a thorough understanding of syntax and data types is crucial. A strong foundation in these concepts allows you to construct reliable programs and avoid common pitfalls. For instance, knowing the difference between mutable variables and immutable constants can prevent subtle bugs in your code. Similarly, understanding how Go treats various data types helps you design efficient programs that perform well even as they scale.

This chapter is divided into several parts. We begin with an overview of the syntax that governs how Go code is written. You will learn about how the language structures programs, the significance of keywords, and the conventions that make Go code readable. Next, we delve into variables and constants—what they are, how they differ, and why you might choose one over the other in different scenarios.

After laying the theoretical groundwork, we shift our focus to data types. In Go, data types include numbers, strings, booleans, and more complex structures such as arrays and slices. Understanding these types is essential because they determine how data is stored, manipulated, and ultimately how it interacts with the computer's memory.

To cement these concepts, this chapter includes a hands-on project that calculates basic statistics. Imagine a scenario where you have a dataset representing a series of measurements—maybe the heights of individuals in a group, or daily sales figures. You will learn to write a program that computes common statistics such as mean, median, and mode. The project not only reinforces your grasp of syntax and data types but also demonstrates practical applications that you can adapt for your own projects.

Throughout this chapter, our tone is clear and supportive. We focus on providing explanations that are straightforward while ensuring that technical terms are defined as soon as they appear. Every concept is illustrated with examples and code snippets that are well-commented and formatted for easy reading. This structure aims to build your confidence step by step as you familiarize yourself with Go.

By the end of this chapter, you will have a solid understanding of Go's basic syntax, the role of variables and constants, and how various data types work together in your programs. You will also gain practical experience by building a statistics calculator—a tool that you can extend or integrate into larger projects in the future.

Let's begin our exploration of Go's syntax and data types, a vital starting point on your path to building robust software systems.

2. Core Concepts and Theory

2.1. The Structure of a Go Program

Every Go program starts with a declaration of its package. The most common package is main, which indicates that the program is executable. In Go, the main function acts as the entry point. This simple structure— declaring a package and writing a main function—keeps programs straightforward and easy to follow.

Imagine a blueprint for a house: the package statement is like laying the foundation, and the main function is the front door where execution begins. This simplicity makes the language accessible to new programmers while still offering the depth needed for complex systems.

Example:

```go
go

package main

import "fmt"

// The main function is the entry point of the
program.
func main() {
    fmt.Println("Welcome to Go!")
}
```

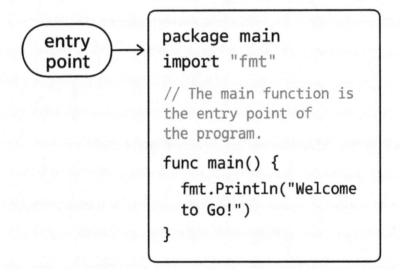

2.2. Keywords, Conventions, and Formatting

Go uses a set of reserved words known as keywords. These words have special meaning in the language and cannot be used as identifiers (names for variables, functions, etc.). Keywords such as if, for, func, var, const, and package form the core language structure. Go's syntax is designed to be unambiguous, promoting consistency and readability.

The language also enforces strict formatting rules. The tool gofmt automatically formats code according to the official style guide, ensuring that code written by different developers maintains a consistent look. This consistency reduces misunderstandings and makes it easier to collaborate on projects.

Common Conventions:

- **Naming:** Use CamelCase for exported functions and variables, and lowerCamelCase for local variables.

- **Indentation:** Use tabs instead of spaces, as enforced by gofmt.

- **Comments:** Comments start with // for single-line comments and /* */ for multi-line comments. Proper commenting is encouraged to improve code readability.

2.3. Variables and Constants

In Go, variables are declared using the var keyword. They can be assigned values at the time of declaration or later in the code. Constants, declared with the const keyword, represent fixed values that cannot change during program execution. Choosing between a variable and a constant depends on whether the data is meant to be mutable.

Variables:

- **Declaration without Initialization:**

```go
var age int
```
Here, age is declared as an integer but not initialized, so it defaults to zero.

- **Declaration with Initialization:**

```go
var score int = 100
```
This initializes score to 100.

- **Short Declaration:**

  In function bodies, you can use the shorthand := operator:

```go
name := "Alice"
```
Constants:

- **Declaration:**

```go
const Pi = 3.14159
```
Constants are useful for values that should not change, such as mathematical constants or configuration values.

Real-World Analogy:

Think of variables as containers that you can refill or change over time, whereas constants are like sealed bottles that always contain the same content.

2.4. Basic Data Types in Go

Go supports several fundamental data types. Here we cover the most important ones:

Numeric Types:

- **Integers:**

  Go provides several integer types (int, int8, int16, int32, int64).

  The type int is platform-dependent.

```go
var count int = 42
```

- **Floating-Point Numbers:**

  Represented by float32 and float64, floating-point numbers store decimal values.

```go
var temperature float64 = 36.6
```

Boolean Type:

- **Booleans:**

  The bool type represents a true or false value.

```go
var isValid bool = true
```

String Type:

- **Strings:**

  In Go, strings are immutable sequences of characters.

```go
var greeting string = "Hello, World!"
```

Composite Types:

- **Arrays:**

  Arrays are fixed-size sequences of elements of a single type.

```go
var numbers [5]int
```

- **Slices:**

    Slices are dynamic, flexible views into arrays.

```go
numbersSlice := []int{1, 2, 3, 4, 5}
```

- **Maps:**

    Maps hold key-value pairs and are useful for fast lookups.

```go
var capitals = map[string]string{
    "France": "Paris",
    "Japan":  "Tokyo",
}
```

Real-World Analogy:

Consider integers and floats like different sizes of measuring cups—each designed to hold certain quantities, while strings are like fixed text messages that you share. Arrays are like fixed-size shelves, slices are adjustable containers, and maps are comparable to dictionaries that match words with definitions.

2.5. Type Conversion and Zero Values

In Go, type conversion is explicit. If you want to convert between types, you must use a conversion function. For example:

```go
var num int = 42
var floatNum float64 = float64(num)
```

Each type also has a zero value (the default value when declared but not initialized). For numbers, this is 0; for booleans, it is false; and for strings, it is an empty string.

2.6. The Importance of Data Types

Understanding data types is fundamental because they determine how data is stored and manipulated. For example, using the wrong data type can lead to unexpected behavior or performance issues. Selecting the appropriate type ensures that your code is both efficient and less prone to errors.

Consider a scenario where you have a large dataset of measurements. If you mistakenly use a type that does not support the required precision, your calculations might be off. This is why paying close attention to data types is crucial.

3. Tools and Setup

Before diving into code examples, ensure that your development environment is properly configured. Although much of the setup has been discussed in earlier chapters, this section focuses on tools relevant to understanding and experimenting with basic syntax and data types in Go.

3.1. Essential Tools for Go Development

For this chapter, you need:

- **The Go Compiler and Runtime:** Installed from the official Go website.

- **A Code Editor or IDE:** Visual Studio Code, GoLand, or another editor with Go support.

- **A Terminal/Command-Line Interface:** To run Go commands.

- **Version Control (Optional):** Git helps manage code changes.

3.2. Configuring Your Editor for Syntax Highlighting

Using an IDE like Visual Studio Code, install the Go extension to benefit from features such as syntax highlighting, auto-completion, and error detection. This will help you see code structure and data types clearly.

Step-by-Step:

1. Open your editor.

2. Navigate to the extensions panel.

3. Search for "Go" and install the official extension.

4. Reload your editor if required.

5. Open a new file (e.g., syntax_demo.go) and observe how keywords and types are highlighted.

3.3. Command-Line Tools

Make sure the Go compiler is accessible through your terminal. Type:

```bash
```

```
go version
```
If the correct version appears, your system is ready for compiling and running code examples. This is critical for experimenting with syntax and data types.

3.4. Using Version Control

While not strictly necessary for understanding syntax, using Git to manage your code is highly recommended. Initialize a repository in your working folder to track changes as you modify examples and build projects.

```bash
```

```
git init
git add .
git commit -m "Initial commit: Basic Syntax and Data Types examples"
```

This practice ensures that you can easily revert to previous versions if needed.

4. Hands-on Examples & Projects

This section brings theory into practice with hands-on examples that progressively build your understanding of Go's syntax and data types. We start with simple examples and then work up to a complete project—a basic statistics calculator.

4.1. Simple Examples of Variables and Constants

Let's start with a basic example that declares several variables and constants and prints their values.

Code Example: Variable and Constant Declarations

```go
package main

import "fmt"

func main() {
    // Declare and initialize variables
    var count int = 10
    var temperature float64 = 98.6
    var isActive bool = true
    var greeting string = "Hello, Go!"

    // Using short declaration syntax
    name := "Developer"
    score := 85

    // Declare constants
    const Pi = 3.14159
    const Language = "Go"

    fmt.Println("Count:", count)
    fmt.Println("Temperature:", temperature)
    fmt.Println("Is Active?", isActive)
    fmt.Println("Greeting:", greeting)
    fmt.Println("Name:", name)
    fmt.Println("Score:", score)
    fmt.Println("Pi:", Pi)
    fmt.Println("Language:", Language)
}
```

Explanation:

This program shows how to declare variables using both the full declaration and shorthand notation. It also demonstrates constant declaration and prints all values to the terminal.

4.2. Working with Basic Data Types

Explore how to work with numbers, strings, booleans, and composite types. The following code illustrates operations on numeric types and string manipulation.

Code Example: Numeric Operations and String Manipulation

```go
package main

import (
    "fmt"
    "strings"
)

func main() {
    // Numeric operations
    var a int = 15
    var b int = 4
    sum := a + b
    diff := a - b
    product := a * b
    quotient := a / b // integer division
    remainder := a % b

    // String operations
    var sentence string = "Go is a powerful language"
    words := strings.Split(sentence, " ")

    fmt.Println("Sum:", sum)
    fmt.Println("Difference:", diff)
    fmt.Println("Product:", product)
    fmt.Println("Quotient:", quotient)
    fmt.Println("Remainder:", remainder)
    fmt.Println("Words in sentence:", words)
```

```
}
```
Explanation:

Here, basic arithmetic operations are performed, and string splitting demonstrates manipulation of textual data. This example reinforces how data types interact with various functions.

4.3. Using Composite Data Types: Arrays, Slices, and Maps

Composite data types are essential for handling collections of data. Below, you see examples that demonstrate the declaration and usage of arrays, slices, and maps.

Code Example: Arrays, Slices, and Maps

```go
package main

import "fmt"

func main() {
    // Array: Fixed-size collection
    var fixedArray [5]int = [5]int{10, 20, 30, 40,
50}
    fmt.Println("Fixed Array:", fixedArray)

    // Slice: Dynamic collection
    dynamicSlice := []string{"apple", "banana",
"cherry"}
    fmt.Println("Dynamic Slice:", dynamicSlice)

    // Map: Key-value store
    capitals := map[string]string{
        "France": "Paris",
        "Spain":  "Madrid",
        "Japan":  "Tokyo",
    }
```

```
    fmt.Println("Capitals Map:", capitals)
}
```

Explanation:

This code shows how to initialize an array, create a slice with string values, and declare a map for country capitals. Each data type is printed to verify its content.

4.4. Hands-on Project: Basic Statistics Calculator

Let's apply these concepts by creating a simple program to calculate basic statistics. Our project will compute the mean, median, and mode for a set of integer values. This example touches on many topics covered so far.

Project Overview

- **Objective:**
  Build a command-line program that reads a list of integers from the user, computes statistical measures, and prints the results.

- **Steps:**

    1. Read input values (as a space-separated string) from the user.

    2. Convert the input into a slice of integers.

    3. Calculate the mean (average), median (middle value), and mode (most frequent value).

    4. Display the results.

Code Example: Basic Statistics Calculator

```go
go

package main

import (
    "bufio"
    "fmt"
    "os"
    "sort"
    "strconv"
    "strings"
)

// calculateMean computes the average of a slice of
integers.
func calculateMean(numbers []int) float64 {
    total := 0
    for _, num := range numbers {
        total += num
    }
    return float64(total) / float64(len(numbers))
}

// calculateMedian computes the median value.
func calculateMedian(numbers []int) float64 {
    sort.Ints(numbers)
    n := len(numbers)
    if n%2 == 0 {
        return float64(numbers[n/2-1]+numbers[n/2]) /
2.0
    }
    return float64(numbers[n/2])
}

// calculateMode computes the mode of a slice of
integers.
func calculateMode(numbers []int) int {
    frequency := make(map[int]int)
    maxCount := 0
    mode := numbers[0]
    for _, num := range numbers {
        frequency[num]++
        if frequency[num] > maxCount {
            maxCount = frequency[num]
```

```go
                mode = num
            }
        }
        return mode
    }

func main() {
    reader := bufio.NewReader(os.Stdin)
    fmt.Print("Enter a list of integers separated by
spaces: ")
    input, _ := reader.ReadString('\n')
    input = strings.TrimSpace(input)
    strNumbers := strings.Split(input, " ")

    var numbers []int
    for _, str := range strNumbers {
        num, err := strconv.Atoi(str)
        if err != nil {
            fmt.Printf("Error: '%s' is not a valid
integer.\n", str)
            return
        }
        numbers = append(numbers, num)
    }

    if len(numbers) == 0 {
        fmt.Println("No numbers provided. Exiting.")
        return
    }

    mean := calculateMean(numbers)
    median := calculateMedian(numbers)
    mode := calculateMode(numbers)

    fmt.Printf("Numbers: %v\n", numbers)
    fmt.Printf("Mean: %.2f\n", mean)
    fmt.Printf("Median: %.2f\n", median)
    fmt.Printf("Mode: %d\n", mode)
}
```

Step-by-Step Explanation:

1. **Input Reading:**

   The program reads a line from standard input, trims whitespace, and splits the string into individual number strings.

2. **Conversion:**

   Each string is converted into an integer using strconv.Atoi. If any conversion fails, an error message is printed.

3. **Calculations:**

   o *Mean:* Sum of numbers divided by the count.

   o *Median:* The middle element after sorting; if even, the average of the two middle elements.

   o *Mode:* The number that appears most frequently.

4. **Output:**

   Results are printed in a clear format.

4.5. Enhancing the Statistics Calculator

Let's extend the project with some additional features:

- **Input Validation:**

  Verify that the user provides valid input.

- **Handling Edge Cases:**

  Address cases like empty input or a list with one element.

- **User Feedback:**

  Print helpful messages to guide the user through corrections if errors occur.

Code Enhancements Example

```go
// Enhanced version with input validation and user
feedback
func main() {
    reader := bufio.NewReader(os.Stdin)
    fmt.Print("Enter a list of integers separated by
spaces: ")
    input, _ := reader.ReadString('\n')
    input = strings.TrimSpace(input)
    if input == "" {
        fmt.Println("No input provided. Please enter
some integers.")
        return
    }
    strNumbers := strings.Split(input, " ")

    var numbers []int
    for _, str := range strNumbers {
        num, err := strconv.Atoi(str)
        if err != nil {
            fmt.Printf("'%s' is not a valid integer.
Please try again.\n", str)
            return
        }
        numbers = append(numbers, num)
    }

    if len(numbers) == 0 {
        fmt.Println("No valid numbers were provided.
Exiting.")
        return
    }

    mean := calculateMean(numbers)
    median := calculateMedian(numbers)
    mode := calculateMode(numbers)

    fmt.Printf("\nStatistics for the input data:\n")
    fmt.Printf("Numbers: %v\n", numbers)
    fmt.Printf("Mean: %.2f\n", mean)
```

```go
        fmt.Printf("Median: %.2f\n", median)
        fmt.Printf("Mode: %d\n", mode)
}
```

Explanation:

Additional checks are introduced to ensure input is not empty and each value is valid. This improves the program's reliability.

4.6. Diagrammatic Representations

Imagine diagrams accompanying the examples:

- **Data Flow Diagram:**
  A block diagram showing how input is taken from the user, passed through a series of functions (mean, median, mode), and then displayed.

- **Directory Structure Diagram:**
  For those who split their code into files, a diagram of the project folder structure (e.g., main file and separate files for helper functions) helps clarify organization.

4.5 . Testing the Statistics Calculator

To ensure our calculator works as expected, it is useful to write test cases. Create a file named statistics_test.go in the same directory as your main program.

Code Example: Testing Functions

```go
go

package main

import "testing"
```

```go
func TestCalculateMean(t *testing.T) {
    nums := []int{10, 20, 30, 40, 50}
    expected := 30.0
    if result := calculateMean(nums); result !=
expected {
        t.Errorf("calculateMean(%v) = %.2f; want
%.2f", nums, result, expected)
    }
}

func TestCalculateMedian(t *testing.T) {
    numsOdd := []int{10, 30, 20}
    expectedOdd := 20.0
    if result := calculateMedian(numsOdd); result !=
expectedOdd {
        t.Errorf("calculateMedian(%v) = %.2f; want
%.2f", numsOdd, result, expectedOdd)
    }

    numsEven := []int{10, 20, 30, 40}
    expectedEven := 25.0
    if result := calculateMedian(numsEven); result !=
expectedEven {
        t.Errorf("calculateMedian(%v) = %.2f; want
%.2f", numsEven, result, expectedEven)
    }
}

func TestCalculateMode(t *testing.T) {
    nums := []int{1, 2, 2, 3, 4}
    expected := 2
    if result := calculateMode(nums); result !=
expected {
        t.Errorf("calculateMode(%v) = %d; want %d",
nums, result, expected)
    }
}
```

Explanation:

These tests verify that each function returns the expected output for given inputs. Run the tests using:

bash

`go test -v`

Testing Functions

Test Case	Input	Expected Output	Actual Result
TestCalculateMean	[10 20 30 40 5]	30.00	30.00
TestCalculateMedian	[10 30 20]	20.00	20.00
TestCalculateMode	[1 2 2 3 4]	2	2

5 . Conclusion & Next Steps

In this chapter, you explored the essential aspects of Go's basic syntax and data types. We began by discussing the overall structure of a Go program and the importance of understanding language keywords and conventions. You learned how variables and constants are declared and used, along with the different data types that Go provides—from numbers and booleans to strings and composite structures like arrays, slices, and maps.

A key takeaway is that a clear understanding of syntax and data types lays the groundwork for writing efficient, maintainable code. By mastering these fundamentals, you are better prepared to tackle more complex problems and build robust applications.

The hands-on project—a basic statistics calculator—served as a practical example of how these concepts come together. From reading user input to converting data and performing calculations, this project not only reinforced your grasp of syntax and data types but also demonstrated how these elements are applied to solve real-world problems.

Looking ahead, consider how you can extend the statistics calculator or integrate it with other projects. Perhaps you might add functionality to handle floating-point numbers, incorporate additional statistical measures, or even build a web interface to display the results. Each extension is an opportunity to deepen your understanding and refine your programming skills.

Your next steps include:

- **Practice and Experiment:**
  Modify the provided examples, try different data types, and see how changes affect your program. Hands-on experimentation is one of the best ways to learn.

- **Further Reading:**
  Explore Go's official documentation and additional tutorials on topics such as composite data types, concurrency, and error handling.

- **Engage with the Community:**
  Join forums, subscribe to newsletters, and participate in coding

challenges. Sharing experiences with other developers can help you overcome challenges and spark new ideas.

Reflect on the concepts covered in this chapter. By carefully working through the basics, you have built a foundation that will support all future learning in Go. The clarity of Go's syntax and the predictability of its data types allow you to focus on solving problems without getting lost in unnecessary complexity.

Thank you for dedicating the time to master these foundational elements. As you continue to explore Go, remember that every piece of code you write, every error you fix, and every project you build contributes to your growth as a developer. With this chapter completed, you are well-equipped to move on to more advanced topics and larger projects.

May your code remain clear, your data well managed, and your programming skills ever expanding.

Chapter 4: Control Structures and Functions

1. Introduction

Control structures and functions are the building blocks that determine how your program makes decisions, iterates over data, and organizes code into reusable units. In this chapter, we explore two essential areas of programming in Go: how to direct the flow of execution using conditionals and loops, and how to encapsulate logic using functions. Whether you are new to programming, have experience in other languages, or enjoy experimenting with code for fun, these topics are key to writing clear, efficient, and maintainable programs.

At its core, every computer program must make decisions based on conditions, repeat actions until tasks are completed, and organize code in a way that makes it easier to manage and reuse. In Go, conditionals (such as if-else statements and switch cases) allow your program to choose different paths during execution. Loops (for loops, in particular) let you repeat operations over collections or until a certain condition is met. These control structures let you express logic that closely mirrors the way you think about real-world processes.

Equally significant are functions, which serve to break your code into smaller, manageable pieces. Functions enable you to group related code together, pass data between parts of your program, and even return results to the calling code. With functions, you not only reduce repetition but also create a structure that is easier to test and maintain. You will see how functions can range from simple helpers that perform arithmetic to more complex routines that manage user input.

Key terminology you will encounter includes "conditional statement," "loop," "iteration," "function declaration," "parameters," and "return values." These terms are common in many programming languages, and understanding them in the context of Go will equip you with skills that are transferable to other environments as well.

Throughout this chapter, you will encounter examples that illustrate how to combine these control structures and functions to build complete, interactive programs. One practical exercise we cover is a command-line tool that interacts with the user—prompting for input, processing that input through loops and conditionals, and organizing the program logic into functions. This example not only demonstrates the syntax but also shows how you might use these constructs in everyday programming tasks.

The content is presented in a professional and approachable tone. Explanations are detailed yet clear, ensuring that beginners can follow along while professionals appreciate the well-structured presentation. As you progress, take note of how conditionals and loops form the decision-making backbone of your applications, and how functions encourage code reuse and modular design. Both concepts are critical when scaling projects, debugging code, or collaborating with others.

By the end of this chapter, you will have a solid understanding of how to use control structures and functions in Go to manage program flow. You will be able to write code that reacts to different conditions, iterates over data efficiently, and organizes complex logic into clear, well-documented functions. With these skills, your programs will not only work correctly but will also be easier to maintain and extend.

Let's now dive into the core concepts, starting with the theory behind control structures and functions, before moving into the practical aspects of writing code that makes decisions and responds to user input.

2. Core Concepts and Theory

2.1. Conditional Statements: Guiding Program Decisions

Conditional statements are the primary means by which your program can take different actions based on the state of its data. In Go, the most common conditional structure is the if-else statement. When a condition is met, the program executes a particular block of code; otherwise, it may execute an alternate block.

The Basic If-Else Statement

Consider the following simple example:

```go
if temperature > 100 {
    fmt.Println("High temperature alert!")
} else {
    fmt.Println("Temperature is within normal
range.")
}
```

In this snippet, the program checks whether the variable temperature exceeds 100. If it does, a warning message is printed. If not, a normal status is displayed. This straightforward decision-making process is essential in situations ranging from monitoring sensor data to validating user input.

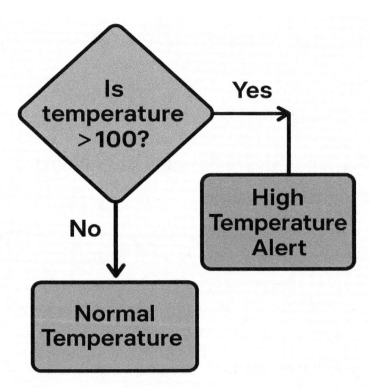

Nested and Else-If Constructs

Sometimes, conditions become more complex. Go allows you to nest if statements or use else if to chain multiple conditions together. For example:

```go
if score >= 90 {
    fmt.Println("Grade: A")
} else if score >= 80 {
    fmt.Println("Grade: B")
} else if score >= 70 {
    fmt.Println("Grade: C")
} else {
    fmt.Println("Grade: D or below")
}
```

Here, the program checks several ranges for a variable score to assign a grade. Such constructs are invaluable when decisions must be made based on multiple factors.

Real-World Analogy:
Think of an academic grading system, where the final mark determines a letter grade. Just as a teacher might have multiple thresholds for different grades, your program uses chained conditionals to decide which message to display.

The Switch Statement

Another powerful tool in Go is the switch statement, which offers an alternative to multiple if-else chains. It compares an expression against multiple values and executes the corresponding case block.

```go
```

```
switch day {
case "Monday":
    fmt.Println("Start of the work week!")
case "Friday":
    fmt.Println("Almost weekend!")
default:
    fmt.Println("Midweek day")
}
```

The switch statement simplifies code when checking a single variable against many potential values. Its structure makes the code more readable and easier to maintain, especially when the alternatives are numerous.

2.2. Loops: Repeating Actions Efficiently

Loops enable your program to perform repetitive tasks without needing to write the same code repeatedly. Go uses the for loop as its sole looping construct, which is versatile enough to cover most iterative needs.

Basic For Loops

A simple for loop in Go might look like this:

```
go
```

```
for i := 0; i < 5; i++ {
    fmt.Println("Iteration:", i)
}
```

This loop initializes i to 0 and then increments it on each iteration, printing the value of i until it reaches 5. Such loops are fundamental when you need to process items in a sequence or repeat an action a fixed number of times.

Real-World Analogy:

Consider a clock ticking every second. Each tick is similar to one iteration of a loop. The loop continues until a specific number of ticks (iterations) has passed.

While-Like Loops in Go

Go does not have a separate while keyword, but you can simulate a while loop by omitting the initialization and post statements:

```go
i := 0
for i < 5 {
    fmt.Println("While-like loop iteration:", i)
    i++
}
```

This style of loop continues to execute as long as the condition is true. It is useful when the number of iterations is not known beforehand.

Infinite Loops and Breaking Out

Sometimes, you need a loop that runs indefinitely until an external condition stops it. In Go, you can write an infinite loop with:

```go
for {
    // Code runs forever unless a break is
encountered
    if conditionMet {
        break
    }
}
```

The break statement exits the loop when a certain condition is met, which is useful in event-driven programming or when processing user input until a termination signal is received.

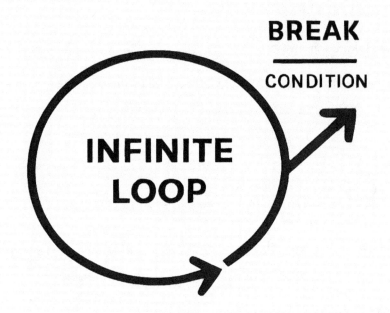

2.3. Functions: Modularizing Code

Functions are used to encapsulate code into self-contained blocks that perform a specific task. They make your code modular and reusable, reducing redundancy and improving clarity.

Declaring and Calling Functions

In Go, functions are declared with the func keyword. Consider the following example:

```go
func add(a int, b int) int {
```

```
        return a + b
}

func main() {
    sum := add(5, 7)
    fmt.Println("Sum:", sum)
}
```

This code defines a simple add function that takes two integers and returns their sum. The main function calls add and prints the result. Notice how the function declaration clearly defines the input parameters and the return type.

Real-World Analogy:

Think of a function as a kitchen appliance like a blender. You put ingredients (parameters) in, and it processes them to give you a smoothie (return value). Once you have the appliance, you can use it over and over without having to rebuild it each time.

Parameters and Return Values

Functions in Go can take multiple parameters and return multiple values. For example:

```go
func divide(numerator, denominator int) (int, int) {
    quotient := numerator / denominator
    remainder := numerator % denominator
    return quotient, remainder
}

func main() {
    q, r := divide(10, 3)
    fmt.Printf("Quotient: %d, Remainder: %d\n", q, r)
}
```

This function, divide, returns both the quotient and remainder of a division operation. Returning multiple values is particularly useful when you need to provide additional context (such as error codes or extra results) from a function.

Function Scope and Lifetime

Variables declared inside a function are local to that function. This encapsulation means that functions do not affect or depend on variables from other parts of the program unless explicitly passed as parameters. This feature promotes code reuse and simplifies debugging.

2.4. Combining Control Structures and Functions

Often, functions and control structures work together to form more sophisticated logic. For instance, you might have a function that processes user input using loops and conditionals to validate data.

Consider this pseudocode structure:

1. A function reads input.

2. Inside the function, a loop continuously prompts the user until valid input is received.

3. Conditional statements evaluate the input and provide feedback.

This pattern is common in command-line applications and graphical interfaces alike.

Real-World Example:

A login function might use a loop to repeatedly prompt the user for credentials until the correct ones are provided, using conditionals to check the entered data and decide whether to grant access or issue a warning.

2.5. Best Practices for Writing Functions and Control Structures

- **Keep Functions Focused:**

  Each function should have a single purpose. Avoid creating "mega-functions" that handle too many tasks.

- **Use Meaningful Names:**

  Name your functions and variables to clearly indicate their purpose. This practice helps others (and your future self) understand your code.

- **Handle Errors Gracefully:**

  When writing functions, particularly those that perform calculations or user input processing, include error handling. This often involves returning an error value alongside the result.

- **Keep Control Structures Simple:**

  Nesting too many conditionals or loops can make code hard to read. Refactor complex logic into helper functions when possible.

3. Tools and Setup

Before you can put these concepts into practice, you need to ensure your environment is ready for development. This section outlines the tools and configurations required for working with control structures and functions in Go.

3.1. Software and Platforms Required

For this chapter, you should have the following:

- **Go Compiler and Runtime:** Installed from the official Go website.

- **An Integrated Development Environment (IDE) or Code Editor:** Visual Studio Code, GoLand, or another editor with Go support.

- **Command-Line Interface:** To run Go programs.

- **Version Control:** Git, for managing your code.

3.2. Configuring Your Code Editor

To benefit from syntax highlighting, code completion, and debugging, it is advisable to configure your editor appropriately. In Visual Studio Code, for example, you can install the Go extension:

1. Open VS Code.

2. Navigate to the Extensions panel.

3. Search for "Go" and install the official extension.

4. Reload the editor if necessary.

5. Open or create a file (e.g., control_functions.go) to see the syntax highlighting in action.

3.3. Command-Line Setup

Ensure that the Go compiler is accessible through your terminal. Open your terminal and type:

```bash
go version
```

If the version is displayed correctly, you are ready to compile and run your programs. This confirmation is essential before moving on to writing your own code.

3.4. Version Control for Code Management

Using Git is recommended for tracking changes and collaborating on projects. Initialize a repository in your working folder:

```bash
git init
git add .
git commit -m "Initial commit: Control Structures and Functions examples"
```

This setup helps you track the evolution of your code and provides a backup if you need to revert changes.

3.5. Project Organization

For clarity, organize your projects into directories. For example, create a folder named go-control-structures with subdirectories for different examples or exercises. This structure keeps your work organized and makes it easier to locate files when needed.

---

4. Hands-on Examples & Projects

This section is dedicated to applying the concepts of control structures and functions through practical examples. We start with simple demonstrations and then build a comprehensive command-line tool that interacts with the user.

4.1. Demonstration of Conditional Statements

Let's start with a basic program that uses an if-else statement to evaluate a condition and print the corresponding message.

Example: Temperature Check

```go
package main

import "fmt"

func main() {
    temperature := 85
    if temperature > 100 {
        fmt.Println("Alert: Temperature is too high!")
    } else {
        fmt.Println("Temperature is within safe limits.")
    }
}
```

Explanation:

This program checks whether the temperature exceeds a set threshold and prints a message accordingly.

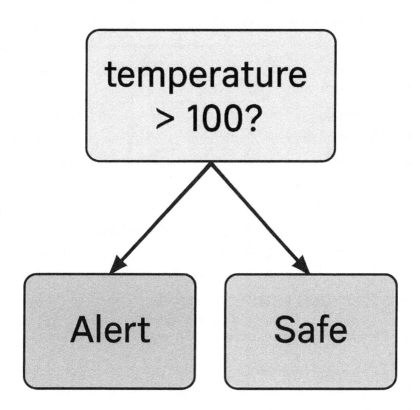

4.2. Using Switch for Multiple Conditions

Next, explore a switch statement to handle several possible values for a variable.

Example: Day of the Week Message

```go
package main

import "fmt"

func main() {
    day := "Wednesday"
    switch day {
    case "Monday":
        fmt.Println("Start of the work week!")
    case "Friday":
        fmt.Println("Almost the weekend!")
    default:
        fmt.Println("Just another day!")
    }
}
```

Explanation:

This program checks the value of day and prints a tailored message. The default case handles any unexpected input.

4.3. Iteration with For Loops

Let's illustrate a basic for loop that iterates a fixed number of times.

Example: Iteration Counter

```go
package main

import "fmt"

func main() {
    for i := 1; i <= 5; i++ {
        fmt.Printf("Iteration %d\n", i)
    }
}
```

Explanation:

The loop prints the current iteration number until it completes five cycles.

4.4. Creating a User Input Loop

Often, programs need to repeatedly prompt for input until a condition is met. The following example simulates a simple login process using a loop.

Example: Password Prompt

```go
package main

import (
    "bufio"
    "fmt"
    "os"
    "strings"
)

func main() {
    correctPassword := "gopass"
    reader := bufio.NewReader(os.Stdin)

    for {
        fmt.Print("Enter password: ")
        input, _ := reader.ReadString('\n')
        input = strings.TrimSpace(input)
        if input == correctPassword {
            fmt.Println("Access granted.")
            break
        } else {
            fmt.Println("Incorrect password. Try again.")
        }
    }
}
```

Explanation:

The program uses a for loop to continuously prompt the user until the correct password is entered. The break statement exits the loop when the condition is satisfied.

4.5. Defining Functions to Encapsulate Logic

Let's now explore how functions help structure your code. We start with a simple function that processes a value and returns a result.

Example: Greeting Function

```go
package main

import "fmt"

// greet takes a name and returns a greeting message.
func greet(name string) string {
    return "Hello, " + name + "!"
}

func main() {
    message := greet("Alex")
    fmt.Println(message)
}
```
Explanation:

This function accepts a name and returns a greeting. The main function then prints this greeting.

4.6. Functions with Multiple Return Values

As an example of functions that return more than one value, consider a function that computes both the quotient and remainder of two integers.

Example: Division Function

```go
package main

import "fmt"

// divide returns the quotient and remainder of two
integers.
func divide(numerator, denominator int) (int, int) {
    quotient := numerator / denominator
    remainder := numerator % denominator
    return quotient, remainder
}

func main() {
    q, r := divide(17, 5)
    fmt.Printf("Quotient: %d, Remainder: %d\n", q, r)
}
```

Explanation:

Here, the function divide processes two integers and returns both the quotient and remainder, demonstrating multiple return values.

4.7. Practical Exercise: Command-Line Tool for User Interaction

In this section, we combine control structures and functions to create a command-line tool that interacts with the user. This project will:

1. Prompt the user for their name.

2. Ask for a numerical input.

3. Process the input through conditional statements.

4. Use functions to calculate and display a message based on the input.

Project Outline:

- **Step 1:** Greet the user and ask for their name.

- **Step 2:** Prompt the user to enter a number.

- **Step 3:** Use a function to evaluate whether the number is even or odd.

- **Step 4:** Display a message based on the evaluation.

- **Step 5:** Loop to allow multiple evaluations until the user opts to exit.

Example Code: Interactive Number Evaluator

```go
package main

import (
    "bufio"
    "fmt"
    "os"
    "strconv"
    "strings"
)

// isEven checks if a number is even.
func isEven(n int) bool {
    return n%2 == 0
}

// evaluateNumber processes the number and returns a message.
func evaluateNumber(n int) string {
```

```go
    if isEven(n) {
        return fmt.Sprintf("The number %d is even.",
n)
    }
    return fmt.Sprintf("The number %d is odd.", n)
}

// promptUser handles reading input from the user.
func promptUser(prompt string) string {
    reader := bufio.NewReader(os.Stdin)
    fmt.Print(prompt)
    input, _ := reader.ReadString('\n')
    return strings.TrimSpace(input)
}

func main() {
    fmt.Println("Welcome to the Interactive Number
Evaluator!")
    for {
        name := promptUser("Enter your name (or type
'exit' to quit): ")
        if strings.ToLower(name) == "exit" {
            fmt.Println("Goodbye!")
            break
        }
        fmt.Printf("Hello, %s!\n", name)

        input := promptUser("Enter an integer: ")
        number, err := strconv.Atoi(input)
        if err != nil {
            fmt.Println("Invalid number. Please try
again.")
            continue
        }

        result := evaluateNumber(number)
        fmt.Println(result)

        again := promptUser("Would you like to
evaluate another number? (yes/no): ")
        if strings.ToLower(again) != "yes" {
            fmt.Println("Thank you for using the
evaluator. Goodbye!")
            break
```

```
        }
        fmt.Println()
    }
}
```

Explanation:

This complete program uses functions to separate concerns: one function to check if a number is even, another to create a message based on that check, and a helper function to prompt the user for input. The main loop ties everything together, allowing repeated interaction until the user types "exit."

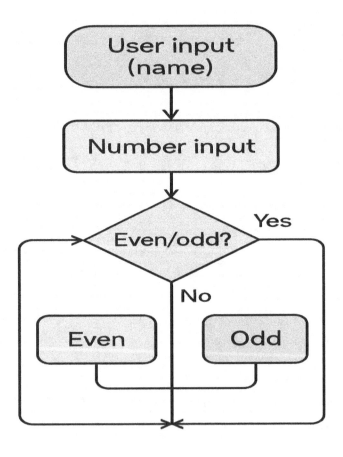

4.8. Enhancing the Tool with Additional Functionality

To further illustrate the power of control structures and functions, you can expand the interactive tool. Consider adding:

- Input validation to handle non-integer values gracefully.

- A menu that allows users to choose different types of evaluations (for example, checking for positivity/negativity or computing the factorial of a number).

- Logging of user interactions to a file for later review.

Example: Extended Interactive Tool

```go
package main

import (
    "bufio"
    "fmt"
    "os"
    "strconv"
    "strings"
)

// isEven checks if a number is even.
func isEven(n int) bool {
    return n%2 == 0
}

// evaluateNumber processes the number and returns a
message about its parity.
func evaluateNumber(n int) string {
    if isEven(n) {
```

```go
        return fmt.Sprintf("The number %d is even.",
n)
    }
    return fmt.Sprintf("The number %d is odd.", n)
}

// evaluateSign returns a message about whether a
number is positive, negative, or zero.
func evaluateSign(n int) string {
    if n > 0 {
        return fmt.Sprintf("The number %d is
positive.", n)
    } else if n < 0 {
        return fmt.Sprintf("The number %d is
negative.", n)
    }
    return "The number is zero."
}

// promptUser handles reading input from the user.
func promptUser(prompt string) string {
    reader := bufio.NewReader(os.Stdin)
    fmt.Print(prompt)
    input, _ := reader.ReadString('\n')
    return strings.TrimSpace(input)
}

func main() {
    fmt.Println("Welcome to the Extended Interactive
Tool!")
    for {
        name := promptUser("Enter your name (or type
'exit' to quit): ")
        if strings.ToLower(name) == "exit" {
            fmt.Println("Goodbye!")
            break
        }
        fmt.Printf("Hello, %s!\n", name)

        // Present a menu of options.
        fmt.Println("Choose an option:")
        fmt.Println("1. Check if a number is even or
odd")
```

```go
        fmt.Println("2. Check if a number is
positive, negative, or zero")
        choice := promptUser("Enter your choice (1 or
2): ")

        input := promptUser("Enter an integer: ")
        number, err := strconv.Atoi(input)
        if err != nil {
            fmt.Println("Invalid number. Please try
again.")
            continue
        }

        switch choice {
        case "1":
            fmt.Println(evaluateNumber(number))
        case "2":
            fmt.Println(evaluateSign(number))
        default:
            fmt.Println("Invalid choice. Please
select 1 or 2.")
            continue
        }

        again := promptUser("Would you like to try
again? (yes/no): ")
        if strings.ToLower(again) != "yes" {
            fmt.Println("Thank you for using the
tool. Goodbye!")
            break
        }
        fmt.Println()
    }
}
```

Explanation:

This version expands the interactive tool by offering a menu and including a new function to evaluate the sign of the number. The use of a switch statement allows easy selection of functionality, further demonstrating control structures.

5. Conclusion & Next Steps

This chapter has provided a comprehensive look at how control structures and functions form the backbone of Go programming. We began by exploring conditional statements and loops, which enable your programs to make decisions and perform repetitive tasks. We then delved into functions, learning how to modularize your code by breaking it into reusable units that accept parameters and return values. These core concepts not only make your code more readable and maintainable but also open the door to building interactive, robust applications.

The hands-on exercises, including the creation of a command-line tool for user interaction, have shown how to put these concepts into practice. By constructing programs that prompt users, process input with loops and conditionals, and use functions to encapsulate logic, you have built a foundation that is applicable to a wide range of projects. These examples are stepping stones toward more complex applications, where the same principles can be scaled and combined with other advanced topics.

Looking ahead, you might consider extending the command-line tool with additional features such as:

- More comprehensive input validation.

- Additional menu options for different types of evaluations.

- Integration with file I/O or network services to handle data in real-world scenarios.

Your next steps include continued practice and exploration. Experiment with modifying the examples provided in this chapter. Try to refactor existing code to improve clarity, add new functions to handle emerging requirements, and write tests to ensure that your code behaves as expected. Over time, these practices will solidify your understanding and make you a more proficient developer.

For further learning, delve into topics such as error handling, concurrency, and package management in Go. The Go documentation and community resources offer a wealth of information and examples that will help you build on what you have learned here.

Reflect on the importance of clear control flow and modular design. As your projects grow in size and complexity, the skills you have developed in this chapter will prove invaluable. Good code is not just about making things work; it is about crafting solutions that are easy to understand, maintain, and expand upon.

Thank you for working through this chapter on control structures and functions. The concepts covered here are essential for any programmer, and mastering them paves the way for tackling more advanced topics in Go. Keep practicing, stay curious, and continue building projects that challenge you to apply these techniques in new and creative ways.

May your code be logical, your functions reusable, and your control flow seamless as you progress in your journey with Go.

Chapter 5: Working with Data Structures

1. Introduction

In any programming language, the ability to store, organize, and manipulate data is essential. In Go, data structures such as arrays, slices, and maps are the fundamental tools for handling collections of data. In this chapter, we explore these structures in detail and explain how you can use them to build efficient and maintainable programs. Whether you're developing applications to manage large datasets or creating simple utilities, understanding these core data structures is critical.

Arrays, slices, and maps are each designed with specific use cases in mind. Arrays are fixed-size collections of elements, providing predictable memory allocation and performance. Slices, built on top of arrays, allow dynamic resizing and are the most commonly used data structure in Go. Maps, on the other hand, are associative arrays that store key-value pairs, making them ideal for tasks such as lookups and indexing.

For many developers, these structures may seem like abstract concepts at first, but they translate directly into everyday programming challenges. Imagine the scenario of keeping track of contacts in an address book. You might use an array or slice to maintain the list of names and a map to quickly search for details by name or phone number. Through clear code examples and practical exercises, this chapter will show you how to design and implement these data structures to suit your needs.

In our hands-on project—a contact list manager—you will apply the concepts learned in this chapter to create an application that stores, retrieves, and updates contact information. This project demonstrates how to combine arrays, slices, and maps to build a tool that is both functional and easy to maintain. In addition, you'll see how organizing your data well leads to simpler code and faster operations, which is critical when scaling up your applications.

Throughout this chapter, the language used is precise and supportive. We define key terms as soon as they appear and provide real-world analogies to make complex ideas accessible. Our approach is to guide you step by step—from understanding the basics of data structures to applying these concepts in a complete project. Whether you are new to programming or an experienced developer, the strategies presented here will help you write cleaner, more effective code.

By the end of this chapter, you should be comfortable with:

- Declaring and initializing arrays, slices, and maps.

- Manipulating these data structures using loops and built-in functions.

- Organizing data in a way that optimizes performance and maintainability.

- Building a complete command-line application—the contact list manager—that demonstrates the practical use of these structures.

Let's begin our journey into Go's data handling capabilities by first examining the core concepts behind arrays, slices, and maps.

---

2. Core Concepts and Theory

In this section, we explore the theory behind arrays, slices, and maps, explaining their purpose, characteristics, and how they fit into Go's overall design philosophy. Understanding these concepts will allow you to choose the right data structure for each task and write programs that are both efficient and easy to understand.

2.1. Arrays: The Building Blocks

Arrays in Go are fixed-length sequences of elements of the same type. When you declare an array, you define its length, and this length cannot change during the array's lifetime. Arrays provide predictable performance since memory allocation is done in a contiguous block. However, their fixed size can be a limitation when you need flexibility.

Definition and Declaration

An array is declared by specifying the type and length. For example:

```go
var numbers [5]int = [5]int{10, 20, 30, 40, 50}
```
This declaration creates an array of five integers. Notice that the length is part of the array's type—[5]int is distinct from [6]int.

Characteristics of Arrays

- **Fixed Length:** Once an array is declared, its length is immutable.

- **Contiguous Memory:** All elements are stored in a continuous block of memory, which can enhance performance in certain scenarios.

- **Value Type:** In Go, arrays are value types. Assigning one array to another copies all elements, which may be inefficient for large arrays.

Real-World Analogy:

Think of an array as an egg carton with a fixed number of slots. No matter how many eggs you want to store later, the carton remains the same size.

2.2. Slices: Flexible and Dynamic

Slices are built on top of arrays but provide a dynamic and flexible way to work with sequences of data. Unlike arrays, slices do not have a fixed size and can grow or shrink as needed. They include a pointer to an underlying array, along with a length and a capacity.

Declaration and Initialization

Slices can be declared using a shorthand notation:

```go
numbersSlice := []int{10, 20, 30, 40, 50}
```

This creates a slice with the same values as an array but with dynamic sizing. You can also create a slice from an existing array:

```go
arr := [5]int{10, 20, 30, 40, 50}
sliceFromArr := arr[1:4]   // Elements at index 1 to 3
```

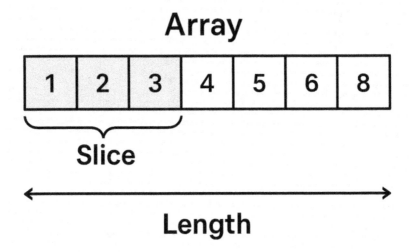

Characteristics of Slices

- **Dynamic Length:** Slices can be resized using built-in functions like append.

- **Reference Type:** Slices reference an underlying array. Changes to a slice may reflect in the original array if they share the same underlying memory.

- **Built-in Functions:** The len function returns the number of elements in a slice, and cap returns its capacity.

Real-World Analogy:

Imagine a flexible notebook where you can add or remove pages as needed. The notebook represents the underlying array, and the visible pages are like a slice that you can adjust.

2.3. Maps: Key-Value Storage

Maps in Go are associative data structures that store pairs of keys and values. They are ideal for tasks where you need fast lookups based on a unique identifier. Maps are implemented as hash tables, offering average-case constant time for lookups, insertions, and deletions.

Declaration and Initialization

A map is declared with the map keyword, specifying the key and value types:

```go
var capitals map[string]string = map[string]string{
    "France": "Paris",
    "Japan":  "Tokyo",
    "Brazil": "Brasília",
}
```
Or using shorthand syntax:

```go
capitals := map[string]string{
    "France": "Paris",
    "Japan":  "Tokyo",
    "Brazil": "Brasília",
}
```

capitals

Country	Capital
France ⟶	Paris
Japan ⟶	Tokyo
Brazil ⟶	Brasília

Characteristics of Maps

- **Unordered:** The order of keys in a map is not guaranteed.

- **Dynamic Size:** Maps can grow as you add more key-value pairs.

- **Reference Type:** Like slices, maps are reference types; they are passed by reference to functions, allowing for in-place updates.

Real-World Analogy:

Think of a map as a dictionary or phone directory, where you look up a person's name (key) to find their phone number (value).

2.4. Organizing and Manipulating Data Effectively

Choosing the right data structure is crucial for writing clear and efficient code. Here are some guiding principles:

- **Use Arrays for Fixed-Size Collections:** When you know the exact number of elements and need fast access without dynamic resizing.

- **Use Slices for Flexible Collections:** When the number of elements may change over time, or when you want to easily take subsets of an array.

- **Use Maps for Quick Lookups:** When you need to retrieve values based on unique keys, such as looking up user details by username.

Combining Data Structures

In many real-world applications, you often need to combine these data structures. For instance, you might store a list of contacts as a slice, and use a map to quickly search for a contact by name. This hybrid approach leverages the strengths of each structure.

Real-World Example:

Imagine an address book: you might use a slice to store all contacts in the order they were added, while a map can help you retrieve a contact's details instantly when you search by name or phone number.

2.5. Memory Considerations

When working with large datasets, it is important to consider the memory footprint of your data structures. Arrays, being fixed-size, have predictable memory usage. Slices, though more flexible, rely on an underlying array whose capacity might exceed the slice's length. Maps, while efficient for lookups, may consume more memory due to their hashing mechanisms.

Understanding these nuances can help you design systems that are both fast and resource-efficient.

---

3. Tools and Setup

Before you begin working with data structures, ensure that your development environment is properly set up. This section outlines the software, editors, and other tools you need to effectively work with arrays, slices, and maps in Go.

3.1. Software Requirements

For this chapter, you need the following:

- **Go Compiler and Runtime:** Download from the official Go website.

- **Integrated Development Environment (IDE) or Text Editor:** Recommended options include Visual Studio Code, GoLand, or Sublime Text.

- **Command-Line Interface:** Terminal on macOS or Linux, or Command Prompt/PowerShell on Windows.

- **Version Control System (Optional):** Git is highly recommended for managing your code changes.

3.2. Installing and Configuring Your Editor

For a smooth coding experience, configure your IDE for Go development. For instance, if you choose Visual Studio Code:

1. Download and install VS Code from code.visualstudio.com.

2. Open the Extensions pane (Ctrl+Shift+X) and search for "Go."

3. Install the official Go extension, which provides syntax highlighting, auto-completion, and debugging features.

4. Reload VS Code if prompted.

5. Open a new file (e.g., datatypes_demo.go) and start coding.

3.3. Command-Line Setup

Ensure that the Go compiler is accessible via your terminal. Open your terminal and type:

```bash
go version
```

A correct output will confirm that Go is installed and ready. This step is crucial before compiling any code examples.

3.4. Version Control Setup

Using Git helps manage your project files and track changes. In your project folder, run:

```bash

git init
git add .
git commit -m "Initial commit: Data Structures examples"
```

This practice will allow you to revert changes if necessary and collaborate with others efficiently.

3.5. Project Organization

Organize your work by creating a dedicated folder for this chapter. For example, create a directory named go-data-structures with subdirectories such as examples, tests, and projects. This structure not only keeps your files tidy but also makes it easier to locate and manage your code as it grows.

4. Hands-on Examples & Projects

This section presents practical examples that build your understanding of data structures in Go. We start with basic demonstrations and progress to a complete project: a contact list manager that stores and retrieves data.

4.1. Basic Examples with Arrays

Let's begin with a simple example that declares and prints an array.

Example: Declaring and Printing an Array

```go
package main

import "fmt"

func main() {
    // Declare an array of 5 integers.
    var numbers [5]int = [5]int{10, 20, 30, 40, 50}
    fmt.Println("Array:", numbers)
}
```

Explanation:

This program declares a fixed-size array of integers and prints its contents. It demonstrates how arrays work and emphasizes their fixed-length property.

4.2. Working with Slices

Now, let's create a slice from an array and demonstrate dynamic resizing using the built-in append function.

Example: Slices and Appending Elements

```go
package main

import "fmt"

func main() {
    // Create a slice of integers.
    numbers := []int{10, 20, 30}
    fmt.Println("Initial Slice:", numbers)

    // Append new elements to the slice.
    numbers = append(numbers, 40, 50)
    fmt.Println("Updated Slice:", numbers)
```

}
Explanation:

This code creates a slice with three elements and then appends two more. It shows how slices offer flexibility by dynamically adjusting their length.

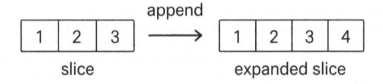

4.3. Utilizing Maps for Key-Value Storage

Next, we illustrate maps with a simple example where we store and retrieve data based on keys.

Example: Basic Map Operations

```go
package main
import "fmt"
func main() {
```

```
    // Create a map that associates countries with
their capitals.
    capitals := map[string]string{
        "France":  "Paris",
        "Japan":   "Tokyo",
        "Brazil":  "Brasília",
    }
    fmt.Println("Capitals Map:", capitals)

    // Retrieve a value from the map.
    capitalOfFrance := capitals["France"]
    fmt.Println("The capital of France is:",
capitalOfFrance)

    // Add a new key-value pair.
    capitals["Germany"] = "Berlin"
    fmt.Println("Updated Map:", capitals)
}
```

Explanation:

This program shows how to declare a map, retrieve values using keys, and add new key-value pairs. It highlights the efficiency of maps in handling associative data.

4.4. Project: Contact List Manager

In this project, you will create a command-line contact list manager that stores, retrieves, updates, and deletes contact information. This project brings together arrays, slices, and maps in a real-world application.

Project Overview

- **Objective:** Build a command-line tool to manage contacts.

- **Features:**

    o   List all contacts.

    o   Add a new contact.

- o   Update an existing contact.

- o   Delete a contact.

- **Data Organization:**

  Use a slice of contacts to maintain order and a map for fast lookups by name or phone number.

Step-by-Step Implementation

Step 1: Define the Contact Structure

Create a new file contact.go to define the contact structure and helper functions.

```go
package contact

// Contact represents an individual contact entry.
type Contact struct {
    ID       int
    Name     string
    Phone    string
    Email    string
}

// NewContact creates a new contact instance.
func NewContact(id int, name, phone, email string)
Contact {
    return Contact{
        ID:    id,
        Name:  name,
        Phone: phone,
        Email: email,
    }
}
```

Explanation:

This code defines a Contact type with basic fields. The helper function
NewContact simplifies creating new contact entries.

Step 2: Manage Contacts with a Manager

In a separate file manager.go, create functions to manage a list of contacts.

```go
package contact

import "errors"

// Manager holds a list of contacts.
type Manager struct {
    Contacts []Contact
    nextID   int
}

// NewManager creates a new Manager instance.
func NewManager() *Manager {
    return &Manager{
        Contacts: []Contact{},
        nextID:   1,
    }
}

// AddContact adds a new contact to the manager.
func (m *Manager) AddContact(name, phone, email
string) {
    contact := NewContact(m.nextID, name, phone,
email)
    m.Contacts = append(m.Contacts, contact)
    m.nextID++
}

// GetContact retrieves a contact by ID.
func (m *Manager) GetContact(id int) (Contact, error)
{
    for _, c := range m.Contacts {
```

```
        if c.ID == id {
            return c, nil
        }
    }
    return Contact{}, errors.New("contact not found")
}

// UpdateContact updates an existing contact.
func (m *Manager) UpdateContact(id int, name, phone,
email string) error {
    for i, c := range m.Contacts {
        if c.ID == id {
            m.Contacts[i].Name = name
            m.Contacts[i].Phone = phone
            m.Contacts[i].Email = email
            return nil
        }
    }
    return errors.New("contact not found")
}

// DeleteContact removes a contact by ID.
func (m *Manager) DeleteContact(id int) error {
    for i, c := range m.Contacts {
        if c.ID == id {
            m.Contacts = append(m.Contacts[:i],
m.Contacts[i+1:]...)
            return nil
        }
    }
    return errors.New("contact not found")
}
```

Explanation:

The Manager type holds a slice of contacts and a counter for the next contact ID. Methods are provided to add, retrieve, update, and delete contacts. Using a slice here preserves the order of contacts, while the methods offer a simple interface for contact management.

Step 3: Create the Command-Line Interface

Finally, build the main application that uses the contact manager. In main.go, write:

```go
package main

import (
    "bufio"
    "fmt"
    "os"
    "strconv"
    "strings"

    "go-data-structures/contact"
)

func prompt(promptText string) string {
    reader := bufio.NewReader(os.Stdin)
    fmt.Print(promptText)
    input, _ := reader.ReadString('\n')
    return strings.TrimSpace(input)
}

func main() {
    manager := contact.NewManager()
    fmt.Println("Welcome to the Contact List
Manager!")

    for {
        fmt.Println("\nMenu:")
        fmt.Println("1. List Contacts")
        fmt.Println("2. Add Contact")
        fmt.Println("3. Update Contact")
        fmt.Println("4. Delete Contact")
        fmt.Println("5. View Contact")
        fmt.Println("6. Exit")
        choice := prompt("Enter your choice: ")

        switch choice {
```

```go
        case "1":
            if len(manager.Contacts) == 0 {
                fmt.Println("No contacts available.")
            } else {
                fmt.Println("Contacts:")
                for _, c := range manager.Contacts {
                    fmt.Printf("ID: %d | Name: %s | Phone: %s | Email: %s\n", c.ID, c.Name, c.Phone, c.Email)
                }
            }
        case "2":
            name := prompt("Enter name: ")
            phone := prompt("Enter phone: ")
            email := prompt("Enter email: ")
            manager.AddContact(name, phone, email)
            fmt.Println("Contact added successfully.")
        case "3":
            idStr := prompt("Enter contact ID to update: ")
            id, err := strconv.Atoi(idStr)
            if err != nil {
                fmt.Println("Invalid ID.")
                continue
            }
            name := prompt("Enter new name: ")
            phone := prompt("Enter new phone: ")
            email := prompt("Enter new email: ")
            if err := manager.UpdateContact(id, name, phone, email); err != nil {
                fmt.Println(err)
            } else {
                fmt.Println("Contact updated successfully.")
            }
        case "4":
            idStr := prompt("Enter contact ID to delete: ")
            id, err := strconv.Atoi(idStr)
            if err != nil {
                fmt.Println("Invalid ID.")
                continue
            }
```

```
            if err := manager.DeleteContact(id); err
!= nil {
                fmt.Println(err)
            } else {
                fmt.Println("Contact deleted
successfully.")
            }
        case "5":
            idStr := prompt("Enter contact ID to
view: ")
            id, err := strconv.Atoi(idStr)
            if err != nil {
                fmt.Println("Invalid ID.")
                continue
            }
            contact, err := manager.GetContact(id)
            if err != nil {
                fmt.Println(err)
            } else {
                fmt.Printf("ID: %d\nName: %s\nPhone:
%s\nEmail: %s\n", contact.ID, contact.Name,
contact.Phone, contact.Email)
            }
        case "6":
            fmt.Println("Exiting Contact List
Manager. Goodbye!")
            return
        default:
            fmt.Println("Invalid choice. Please try
again.")
        }
    }
}
```
Explanation:

The main application offers a menu-driven command-line interface. It uses helper functions to prompt the user and then calls methods on the Manager to perform operations. The switch statement cleanly dispatches user choices to corresponding actions.

4.5. Testing the Contact List Manager

To ensure the contact list manager works as intended, write tests for key functions in the contact package. Create a file named manager_test.go:

```go
package contact

import "testing"

func TestAddAndGetContact(t *testing.T) {
    mgr := NewManager()
    mgr.AddContact("Alice", "1234567890",
"alice@example.com")
    contact, err := mgr.GetContact(1)
    if err != nil {
        t.Fatalf("Expected contact to be found, got
error: %v", err)
    }
    if contact.Name != "Alice" {
        t.Errorf("Expected name 'Alice', got '%s'",
contact.Name)
    }
}

func TestUpdateContact(t *testing.T) {
    mgr := NewManager()
    mgr.AddContact("Bob", "0987654321",
"bob@example.com")
    err := mgr.UpdateContact(1, "Bobby",
"0987654321", "bobby@example.com")
    if err != nil {
        t.Fatalf("UpdateContact failed: %v", err)
    }
    contact, _ := mgr.GetContact(1)
    if contact.Name != "Bobby" {
        t.Errorf("Expected updated name 'Bobby', got
'%s'", contact.Name)
    }
}
```

```
func TestDeleteContact(t *testing.T) {
    mgr := NewManager()
    mgr.AddContact("Carol", "5555555555",
"carol@example.com")
    err := mgr.DeleteContact(1)
    if err != nil {
        t.Fatalf("DeleteContact failed: %v", err)
    }
    _, err = mgr.GetContact(1)
    if err == nil {
        t.Error("Expected error when retrieving
deleted contact, got nil")
    }
}
```

Explanation:

These tests validate the core functionalities of the contact manager, ensuring that adding, updating, and deleting contacts work as expected.

---

5 . Conclusion & Next Steps

Throughout this chapter, you have explored the foundations of working with data structures in Go. We began by examining the characteristics of arrays, slices, and maps—understanding their strengths and limitations, and how they can be used to efficiently store and retrieve data. With real-world analogies, clear definitions, and code examples, the core concepts have been made accessible for newcomers while still providing depth for experienced programmers.

The contact list manager project served as a capstone, demonstrating how to combine these data structures in a practical application. You learned to design a system that maintains a list of contacts, offering features such as adding, updating, deleting, and viewing contacts. This project not only reinforces the theory behind data structures but also illustrates the importance of good data organization in application design.

Looking ahead, consider the following steps to further enhance your skills:

- **Experiment with Modifications:**
  Try adding new features to the contact list manager, such as sorting contacts, filtering by criteria, or even integrating with a database.

- **Study Advanced Data Handling:**
  Explore more complex data structures like linked lists, trees, and graphs if your projects require them.

- **Engage with the Community:**
  Review open-source projects written in Go to see how others structure and optimize their data management code.

- **Practice Profiling:**
  Use tools like pprof to analyze the performance of your code, especially when dealing with large datasets.

Reflect on how the thoughtful organization of data structures can simplify your code and improve performance. As your applications become more complex, the principles of clean data management you've learned here will continue to serve you well.

Thank you for working through this chapter. The skills and concepts covered—from understanding arrays, slices, and maps to applying them in a real-world project—are key building blocks in your journey as a Go developer. Continue practicing, refining your techniques, and exploring additional resources to further deepen your understanding.

May your code remain organized, your data well managed, and your applications scalable as you apply these principles to ever more challenging projects.

Chapter 6: Pointers, Structs, and Interfaces

1. Introduction

In programming, one of the most challenging yet rewarding skills is mastering how data is managed and organized in memory. In Go, pointers, structs, and interfaces form a trio that empowers you to write efficient and modular code. This chapter is dedicated to exploring these topics in detail.

Imagine you have a toolbox. Pointers are like a pair of pointers that let you refer to tools stored in different drawers without moving them around. Structs are custom-made tool organizers that help you group related tools together, while interfaces are like standardized labels that ensure any tool, regardless of its make or model, can be used interchangeably if it meets a particular specification.

Understanding pointers is essential because they provide direct access to memory. This means you can work with data more efficiently and even manipulate it in place. However, pointers come with their own set of challenges, such as avoiding unintended modifications and managing memory safely. Throughout this chapter, we'll see how Go simplifies pointer usage compared to languages like C, yet retains the power to boost performance and fine-tune memory management.

Structs, on the other hand, let you create complex data types by grouping together fields that share a common theme. Whether you're building a user profile, a configuration setting, or a representation of a real-world object, structs allow you to organize data in a clear, logical way. They are the backbone of many Go applications, offering a level of structure that makes code both maintainable and scalable.

Finally, interfaces in Go provide a way to define behavior. They allow you to write functions and methods that can operate on a variety of types as long as they adhere to a defined set of methods. This opens the door to flexible and reusable code design. Instead of tying your functions to a specific type, interfaces let you define contracts that any type can fulfill. This makes your code more abstract, decoupled, and easier to test.

In this chapter, we begin with an introduction to pointers. We explain what they are, how they work, and why they're useful, including discussions of memory addresses and dereferencing. Then we move on to structs, discussing how to define them, initialize them, and use them to model real-world data. We also cover methods—functions that are associated with structs—which further extend the power of data organization.

Afterwards, we explore interfaces. You'll learn how to define an interface, how types implement interfaces implicitly, and how to leverage interfaces to create flexible designs. A key takeaway is that interfaces allow you to write functions that can operate on any type that meets a given contract, making your code highly reusable and adaptable.

To cement these concepts, the chapter includes a hands-on project: a basic simulation that uses both structs and interfaces. In this project, you'll build a simulation of a simple ecosystem. For example, you might model different animals (using structs) and define behaviors (via interfaces) such as "move" or "makeSound." By designing your simulation with interfaces, you can add new types of animals without changing the code that uses them—a powerful demonstration of polymorphism in action.

Throughout the chapter, the tone remains professional and engaging. Concepts are introduced step by step, with real-world analogies that simplify complex ideas. Code examples are cleanly formatted and well-commented to ensure that both beginners and experienced programmers can follow along.

By the end of this chapter, you will have gained a deep understanding of how pointers, structs, and interfaces work in Go. You'll be able to manage memory more efficiently, design well-organized data structures, and write code that is flexible enough to adapt to future changes. Whether you are building small utilities or large-scale applications, these concepts are fundamental to writing robust, maintainable software.

Let's embark on this exploration of memory management and data organization in Go. We will start by examining pointers in detail, and then proceed to build upon that knowledge as we explore structs and interfaces.

2. Core Concepts and Theory

2.1. Pointers and Memory Management

Pointers provide a way to reference memory directly. In Go, a pointer is a variable that holds the memory address of another variable. This ability to refer to memory locations directly can greatly enhance performance, especially when dealing with large data structures or passing data between functions.

2.1.1. Understanding Pointers

A pointer is declared using an asterisk (*) before the type. For example, the declaration var p *int indicates that p is a pointer to an integer. To obtain the memory address of a variable, you use the ampersand (&) operator.

Example:

```go
go

package main

import "fmt"

func main() {
    var num int = 42
    var ptr *int = &num  // ptr holds the address of
num
    fmt.Println("Value of num:", num)
    fmt.Println("Address of num:", ptr)
}
```

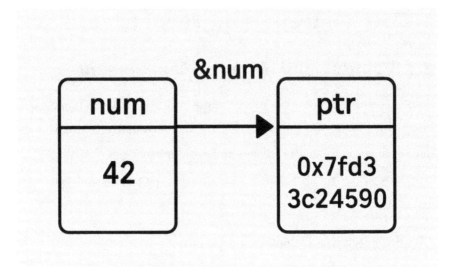

2.1.2. Dereferencing Pointers

Dereferencing a pointer means accessing the value stored at the memory address the pointer references. In Go, this is done by prefixing the pointer variable with an asterisk.

Example:

```go
package main

import "fmt"

func main() {
    var num int = 42
    var ptr *int = &num
    fmt.Println("Dereferenced value:", *ptr)  // Output: 42
}
```

Here, *ptr returns the value stored at the memory location pointed to by ptr. This technique is crucial for manipulating data indirectly.

2.1.3. Pointers in Function Arguments

One major use of pointers is to pass large data structures to functions without ing the entire structure. By passing a pointer, you allow the function to modify the original variable.

Example:

```go
package main

import "fmt"

func increment(num *int) {
    *num++  // Dereference and increment the value
}

func main() {
    value := 10
    increment(&value)
    fmt.Println("Incremented value:", value)
}
```

Real-World Analogy:

Think of a pointer as a remote control that allows you to change the channel on a TV without physically touching it. The remote (pointer) sends signals to the TV (variable) to change its state.

2.1.4. Benefits and Caveats of Pointers

Pointers can optimize memory usage and performance but must be used carefully. Unintended modifications, dangling pointers (pointers referencing deallocated memory), or nil pointers can lead to bugs. Go's garbage collection helps manage memory, but understanding pointers is still essential for writing high-performance code.

2.2. Structs: Defining Custom Data Types

Structs in Go are composite data types that group together fields with varying data types. They provide a way to model complex data entities and are central to Go's approach to organizing code.

2.2.1. Declaring and Initializing Structs

A struct is declared using the type keyword, followed by a name and a collection of fields enclosed in braces.

Example:

```go
package main

import "fmt"

// Define a struct representing a person.
type Person struct {
    Name string
    Age  int
    Email string
}

func main() {
    // Initialize a struct using a literal.
    person := Person{
        Name: "Alice",
        Age:  30,
        Email: "alice@example.com",
    }
    fmt.Println("Person:", person)
}
```

Visual Aid Description:

Visualize a box labeled "Person" with compartments for Name, Age, and Email. Each compartment holds a corresponding value.

2.2.2. Structs and Memory

Structs are allocated as contiguous blocks of memory, which makes access fast and predictable. They can be passed by value (ing the entire struct) or by pointer (referencing the same memory).

2.2.3. Methods on Structs

In Go, you can attach methods to structs. This is done by defining functions with a receiver argument that specifies the struct type.

Example:

```go
package main

import "fmt"

// Define the Person struct.
type Person struct {
    Name string
    Age  int
}

// Method to display the person's details.
func (p Person) Greet() {
    fmt.Printf("Hello, my name is %s and I am %d
years old.\n", p.Name, p.Age)
}

func main() {
    person := Person{"Bob", 25}
    person.Greet()
```

}

Here, the Greet method is associated with the Person struct, encapsulating behavior along with data.

2.2.4. Structs for Data Organization

Structs help organize related data, making your code modular and easier to maintain. In real-world applications, structs can represent entities such as customers, products, or even configuration settings.

Real-World Analogy:

Think of a struct as a record in a database. Each record holds fields like name, age, or address. Structs similarly bundle related data together.

2.3. Interfaces: Defining Behavior

Interfaces in Go define a set of method signatures that any type can implement. They provide a way to write flexible, decoupled code where functions can operate on different types as long as they implement the required methods.

2.3.1. Declaring Interfaces

An interface is declared using the type keyword. It lists the methods that must be implemented.

Example:

```go
package main

import "fmt"
```

```go
// Define an interface for printable objects.
type Printable interface {
    PrintInfo()
}
```
Any type that implements the PrintInfo method automatically satisfies the Printable interface.

2.3.2. Implementing Interfaces

Types implement interfaces implicitly. There is no need to declare that a type implements an interface; it's enough that the type defines the required methods.

Example:

```go
go

package main

import "fmt"

// Define the Printable interface.
type Printable interface {
    PrintInfo()
}

// Define a struct.
type Person struct {
    Name string
    Age  int
}

// Implement PrintInfo on Person.
func (p Person) PrintInfo() {
    fmt.Printf("Name: %s, Age: %d\n", p.Name, p.Age)
}

func main() {
    var p Printable = Person{"Carol", 28}
    p.PrintInfo()
```

}
Real-World Analogy:

Imagine an interface as a job description that outlines responsibilities. Any employee (type) that can perform those duties (methods) is qualified (implements the interface), regardless of their background.

2.3.3. Benefits of Interfaces

Interfaces promote flexible code design by decoupling the definition of behavior from specific implementations. They allow you to write functions that work with any type that satisfies the interface, enabling polymorphism and easier testing.

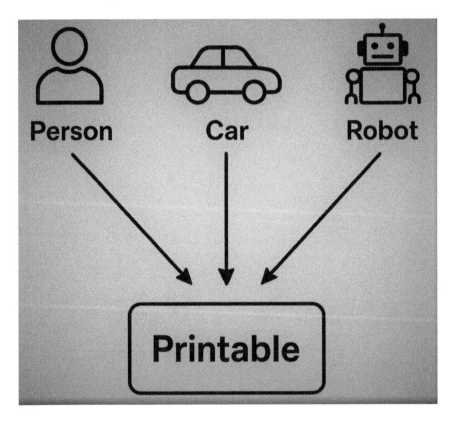

2.4. Putting It All Together: A Basic Simulation

To illustrate how pointers, structs, and interfaces work in concert, let's consider a simple simulation. In this simulation, we model a basic ecosystem where different types of creatures implement a common behavior. We define structs to represent creatures, use pointers for efficient memory handling, and employ an interface to define common actions like "Move" or "Speak."

Simulation Overview

Imagine a simulation with two types of creatures: a "Dog" and a "Cat." Both types will implement an interface called Animal that requires a method Speak(). We will also see how pointers can be used when passing data to functions that modify a creature's state (like updating its age).

Real-World Example:
The simulation resembles a small pet management system where each animal has attributes (name, age) and behaviors (speak, move). The flexibility of interfaces allows you to add new animal types later without modifying the system's core logic.

---

3. Tools and Setup

Before diving into coding, ensure that your environment is set up to support pointers, structs, and interfaces in Go. This section details the tools you'll need and how to configure them.

3.1. Required Software

For this chapter, you need:

- **Go Compiler and Runtime:** Available from the official Go website.

- **Integrated Development Environment (IDE) or Code Editor:** Options like Visual Studio Code, GoLand, or Sublime Text.

- **Command-Line Interface:** Terminal on macOS/Linux or Command Prompt/PowerShell on Windows.

- **Version Control:** Git, to manage code changes.

3.2. Installing and Configuring the IDE

For a smooth experience, configure your IDE for Go development:

1. **Install the IDE:** Download and install Visual Studio Code from code.visualstudio.com or your preferred editor.

2. **Install the Go Extension:** Open the Extensions pane (Ctrl+Shift+X in VS Code), search for "Go," and install the official extension.

3. **Configure Settings:** Ensure your editor is set to use gofmt for code formatting and to provide syntax highlighting for Go code.

4. **Create a Workspace:** Organize your files by creating a dedicated folder (e.g., go-pointers-structs-interfaces).

3.3. Command-Line Configuration

Verify that the Go compiler is correctly installed by opening a terminal and running:

bash

```
go version
```
The output should confirm the version of Go installed. This step is crucial before you compile any code examples.

3.4. Version Control Setup

Initialize a Git repository in your workspace to track your progress and manage changes:

bash

```
git init
git add .
git commit -m "Initial commit: Pointers, Structs, and
Interfaces chapter setup"
```
This helps you revert changes if necessary and collaborate with others if you're working in a team.

3.5. Project Organization

For clarity and maintainability, organize your code into multiple files and directories:

- **/cmd:** For command-line application entry points.

- **/pkg:** For reusable packages like your simulation or helper functions.

- **/test:** For unit tests of your functions.

---

4. Hands-on Examples & Projects

In this section, we apply our understanding of pointers, structs, and interfaces through practical examples and projects. We start with simple demonstrations and gradually build to a complete simulation project.

4.1. Simple Pointer Examples

Let's begin with a straightforward demonstration of pointers. This example shows how to declare, assign, and dereference pointers.

Example: Basic Pointer Usage

```go
package main

import "fmt"

func main() {
    var number int = 100
    var ptr *int = &number  // ptr holds the memory address of number
    fmt.Println("Value of number:", number)
    fmt.Println("Memory address stored in ptr:", ptr)
    fmt.Println("Dereferenced value:", *ptr)
}
```

Explanation:

This code explains how to create a pointer, assign it the address of a variable, and then dereference it to access the variable's value. The output confirms that both the direct value and the dereferenced pointer produce the same result.

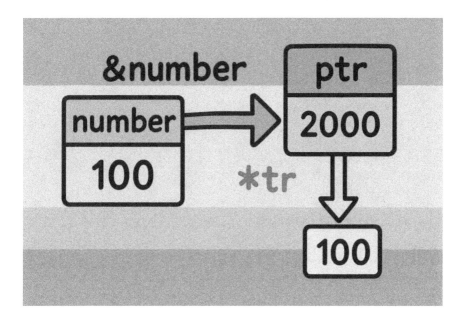

4.2. Defining and Using Structs

Now, we'll create a simple struct to represent an entity—such as a "Car."
This example demonstrates how to define a struct, initialize it, and access
its fields.

Example: Car Struct

```go
package main

import "fmt"

// Define a struct for a Car.
type Car struct {
    Make  string
    Model string
    Year  int
}
```

```
// Method to display car information.
func (c Car) DisplayInfo() {
    fmt.Printf("Car: %s %s, Year: %d\n", c.Make,
c.Model, c.Year)
}

func main() {
    // Initialize a Car instance.
    myCar := Car{
        Make:   "Toyota",
        Model: "Corolla",
        Year:   2020,
    }
    myCar.DisplayInfo()
}
```

Explanation:

This code defines a Car struct with three fields and a method DisplayInfo that prints the car's details. The example demonstrates how to encapsulate data and behavior together in a single unit.

4.3. Pointers with Structs

You can also work with pointers to structs to avoid ing data and to enable modifications to the original object.

Example: Updating a Struct via a Pointer

```go
go

package main

import "fmt"

// Define a Person struct.
type Person struct {
    Name string
    Age   int
}

// Method to update the person's age.
```

```go
func (p *Person) UpdateAge(newAge int) {
    p.Age = newAge
}

func main() {
    person := Person{"David", 30}
    fmt.Printf("Before update: %+v\n", person)
    person.UpdateAge(31)
    fmt.Printf("After update: %+v\n", person)
}
```
Explanation:

Here, UpdateAge is defined with a pointer receiver, allowing the method to modify the original Person instance rather than a .

4.4. Introducing Interfaces

Let's now explore interfaces by creating an interface for a simple simulation. Define an interface named Mover that requires a method Move().

Example: Mover Interface and Animal Structs

```go
package main

import "fmt"

// Mover interface requires a Move method.
type Mover interface {
    Move() string
}

// Dog struct.
type Dog struct {
    Name string
}

// Cat struct.
type Cat struct {
```

```
    Name string
}

// Implement Move for Dog.
func (d Dog) Move() string {
    return d.Name + " runs swiftly."
}

// Implement Move for Cat.
func (c Cat) Move() string {
    return c.Name + " leaps gracefully."
}

func main() {
    var mover Mover
    mover = Dog{Name: "Buddy"}
    fmt.Println(mover.Move())

    mover = Cat{Name: "Whiskers"}
    fmt.Println(mover.Move())
}
```

Explanation:

This example shows how both Dog and Cat types implement the Mover
interface implicitly by defining a Move method. The code demonstrates
polymorphism, where the same interface variable can hold different types
that satisfy the interface.

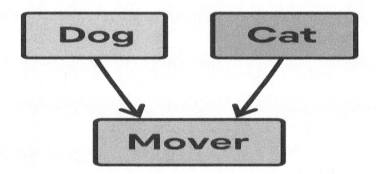

4.5. Building a Simulation: A Basic Ecosystem

Now we combine pointers, structs, and interfaces in a hands-on project. In this simulation, we model an ecosystem with different creatures that move and speak. We'll define a general interface called Animal with methods like Speak() and Move(), then create several structs (e.g., Dog, Cat, Bird) that implement these methods.

Project Outline

- **Define the Animal Interface:**
  The interface includes Speak() and Move() methods.

- **Create Structs for Different Animals:**
  Each animal struct has fields like Name and Age and implements the interface.

- **Use Pointers to Manage Animals:**
  Create a slice of pointers to Animal (or to the concrete types) to simulate interactions.

- **Simulation Loop:**
  Write a loop that iterates over the animals, calling their methods and printing the results.

Step-by-Step Implementation

Step 1: Define the Animal Interface and Structs

```go
package ecosystem
```

```go
import "fmt"

// Animal interface defines behaviors.
type Animal interface {
    Speak() string
    Move() string
}

// Dog struct representing a dog.
type Dog struct {
    Name string
    Age  int
}

// Cat struct representing a cat.
type Cat struct {
    Name string
    Age  int
}

// Bird struct representing a bird.
type Bird struct {
    Name string
    Age  int
}

// Implement Speak and Move for Dog.
func (d Dog) Speak() string {
    return fmt.Sprintf("%s barks: Woof!", d.Name)
}
func (d Dog) Move() string {
    return fmt.Sprintf("%s runs energetically.",
d.Name)
}

// Implement Speak and Move for Cat.
func (c Cat) Speak() string {
    return fmt.Sprintf("%s meows: Meow!", c.Name)
}
func (c Cat) Move() string {
    return fmt.Sprintf("%s prowls silently.", c.Name)
}

// Implement Speak and Move for Bird.
```

```go
func (b Bird) Speak() string {
    return fmt.Sprintf("%s chirps: Tweet!", b.Name)
}
func (b Bird) Move() string {
    return fmt.Sprintf("%s flies gracefully.",
b.Name)
}
```

Step 2: Create a Simulation Program

```go
go

package main

import (
    "fmt"
    "go-pointers-structs-interfaces/ecosystem"
)

func main() {
    // Create a slice of Animal interfaces.
    animals := []ecosystem.Animal{
        ecosystem.Dog{Name: "Rex", Age: 5},
        ecosystem.Cat{Name: "Misty", Age: 3},
        ecosystem.Bird{Name: "Tweety", Age: 2},
    }

    fmt.Println("Ecosystem Simulation:")
    for _, animal := range animals {
        fmt.Println(animal.Speak())
        fmt.Println(animal.Move())
        fmt.Println("-----")
    }
}
```

Explanation:

This program sets up a simple ecosystem by creating different animal objects and storing them in a slice of the Animal interface. The simulation loop iterates through the slice, invoking each animal's Speak() and Move() methods.

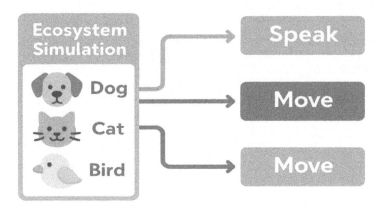

4.6. Extending the Simulation with Pointers

Using pointers in the simulation can allow dynamic updates to each animal's state (for example, aging or position updates). Below is an enhanced version where each animal is managed via a pointer.

Example: Enhanced Simulation with Pointers

```go
go

package main

import (
    "fmt"
    "go-pointers-structs-interfaces/ecosystem"
)

func main() {
    // Create a slice of pointers to Animal objects.
    animals := []ecosystem.Animal{
        &ecosystem.Dog{Name: "Rex", Age: 5},
        &ecosystem.Cat{Name: "Misty", Age: 3},
        &ecosystem.Bird{Name: "Tweety", Age: 2},
```

```go
    }

    fmt.Println("Enhanced Ecosystem Simulation:")
    for _, animal := range animals {
        fmt.Println(animal.Speak())
        fmt.Println(animal.Move())
        fmt.Println("-----")
    }
}
```

Explanation:

Here, we store pointers to our animal objects. This allows any modifications (if methods were to change internal state) to be reflected outside the function call, and is more efficient for larger structures.

4.7. Project Wrap-Up and Testing

After building the simulation, test each component separately:

- **Unit Test for Each Animal Type:**
  Write tests to ensure that Speak() and Move() return expected strings.

- **Integration Test:**
  Verify that the simulation loop correctly iterates through the slice and calls methods on each animal.

Example: Unit Test for Dog's Methods

```go
package ecosystem

import "testing"

func TestDogSpeak(t *testing.T) {
    dog := Dog{Name: "Buddy", Age: 4}
    expected := "Buddy barks: Woof!"
```

```
    if dog.Speak() != expected {
        t.Errorf("Expected '%s', got '%s'", expected,
dog.Speak())
    }
}

func TestDogMove(t *testing.T) {
    dog := Dog{Name: "Buddy", Age: 4}
    expected := "Buddy runs energetically."
    if dog.Move() != expected {
        t.Errorf("Expected '%s', got '%s'", expected,
dog.Move())
    }
}
```

Explanation:

These tests confirm that the Dog struct's methods work as intended.

Similar tests can be written for Cat and Bird.

---

5 . Conclusion & Next Steps

In this chapter, we explored three fundamental aspects of Go that enable efficient memory management and flexible design: pointers, structs, and interfaces. We began by explaining pointers—their syntax, usage, and benefits—illustrating how direct memory access can improve performance. We then moved on to structs, learning how to define custom data types that organize related information. Next, we examined interfaces, showing how they define behavior and promote a flexible, decoupled design.

The hands-on project—a basic simulation of an ecosystem—demonstrated how these concepts work together. By modeling different animals using structs and allowing them to behave polymorphically through interfaces, you saw firsthand how to design code that is both modular and extensible.

Advanced topics such as embedding, interface composition, and performance optimizations further rounded out your understanding and provided strategies for tackling real-world challenges.

Looking ahead, here are your next steps:

- **Practice Extensively:**
  Modify the simulation, add new animal types, or incorporate additional behaviors. The more you practice, the more intuitive these concepts will become.

- **Explore Further Resources:**
  The official Go documentation, online tutorials, and community forums offer endless opportunities for deeper exploration of pointers, structs, and interfaces.

- **Integrate Advanced Patterns:**
  Experiment with design patterns that utilize interfaces and pointers to build scalable, maintainable systems. Consider studying patterns like dependency injection and the strategy pattern.

- **Keep Testing:**
  Write unit tests and benchmarks for your functions and methods. Testing not only ensures correctness but also helps in identifying performance bottlenecks.

Reflect on the importance of these concepts in your development journey. Pointers provide control over memory and performance, structs bring order to data, and interfaces allow your code to adapt to change. Mastering these topics opens up a realm of possibilities—from low-level optimizations to high-level design patterns.

Thank you for working through this chapter on pointers, structs, and interfaces. The skills you've developed here are indispensable for writing robust, efficient, and scalable Go programs. As you continue to build larger and more complex applications, remember that a deep understanding of how data is stored, organized, and manipulated will always be at the heart of great software design.

May your pointers always point correctly, your structs remain well-organized, and your interfaces provide the flexibility needed to build amazing applications. Happy coding, and best of luck on your continued journey with Go!

Chapter 7: Concurrency Essentials

1. Introduction

In today's computing landscape, the ability to perform multiple operations at once is no longer a luxury—it's a necessity. Concurrency allows your programs to make full use of modern multi-core processors, leading to better performance and responsiveness. In Go, concurrency is a first-class citizen. The language provides lightweight constructs called goroutines that let you perform tasks simultaneously with minimal overhead.

This chapter is dedicated to exploring concurrency essentials in Go. We begin by defining key concepts such as concurrency, parallelism, and the difference between them. You'll learn why concurrent programming is critical for developing scalable, efficient, and responsive applications. Whether you are a beginner new to concurrent programming, a professional looking to refine your skills, or a hobbyist interested in experimenting with parallel tasks, this chapter will offer valuable insights.

We will discuss how goroutines work, including how they are created and managed by the Go runtime. You'll see how the simplicity of starting a goroutine (just by prepending the keyword go to a function call) hides powerful underpinnings that enable complex concurrency patterns.

Alongside goroutines, we'll briefly touch on the role of channels, which provide a safe way to communicate between concurrent tasks. While our primary focus will be on goroutines, you'll gain an appreciation for how these pieces fit together in a real-world program.

The chapter is structured to build your understanding progressively. We begin with an overview of concurrency concepts and key terminology. Next, we dive into the theory behind goroutines and explain how they differ from traditional threads in other languages. We then cover the tools and setup needed to write and test concurrent programs in Go, ensuring that your development environment is ready for the challenges ahead.

Following the theory, the heart of the chapter is a hands-on project. You will build a small command-line program that handles multiple operations at once. This project will illustrate how to start goroutines, manage their execution, and coordinate their outputs. By the end of the project, you'll see practical examples of how concurrent programming can make your applications faster and more responsive.

Throughout the chapter, the tone remains professional and engaging. Explanations are detailed yet accessible, and every technical term is defined and illustrated with real-world examples. Code snippets are cleanly formatted and well-commented to ensure that you can follow the logic step by step. Diagrams and screenshots—described in detail here—help visualize how goroutines are scheduled and how they interact within your program.

By the end of this chapter, you will understand the essentials of concurrency in Go and be able to write programs that perform multiple operations simultaneously. You'll appreciate the power and elegance of goroutines and be prepared to apply these techniques to your own projects, whether you're developing web servers, real-time applications, or any software that demands high performance.

Let's now embark on our journey into the world of concurrent programming in Go, starting with the foundational concepts and moving toward practical applications.

---

2. Core Concepts and Theory

Concurrency in Go is built around several key ideas that differentiate it from traditional threading models. In this section, we break down the core concepts and provide real-world analogies to make these ideas accessible.

2.1. Defining Concurrency and Parallelism

Concurrency means that multiple tasks are in progress at the same time. This doesn't necessarily mean that they are executing simultaneously (that's parallelism), but rather that they are managed in a way that makes progress on multiple tasks appear to overlap.

Parallelism, on the other hand, is the physical execution of multiple tasks at the same time, often on multiple cores or processors. In Go, goroutines allow you to write concurrent programs that may also run in parallel, depending on the hardware and Go's scheduler.

Real-World Analogy:
Imagine you're in a busy kitchen. Concurrency is like having multiple dishes in preparation—while one dish simmers, you might chop vegetables

for another. Parallelism is when two chefs work simultaneously on different dishes. Even if you're the only chef (single-threaded), you can still start tasks that allow the oven to do its work while you continue chopping, which is concurrency.

2.2. The Role of Goroutines

Goroutines are the lightweight threads of execution in Go. They are incredibly cheap to create compared to traditional OS threads. You can start thousands of goroutines without worrying about resource constraints.

2.2.1. Creating a Goroutine

To start a goroutine, simply use the go keyword before a function call:

```
go
```

```
go someFunction()
```
This line tells the Go runtime to execute someFunction() concurrently with the rest of the program. The simplicity of this syntax is one of Go's greatest strengths.

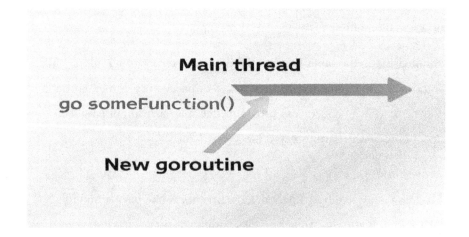

2.2.2. Scheduling and Execution

Goroutines are managed by Go's scheduler, which multiplexes them onto a smaller number of operating system threads. This scheduler is responsible for deciding which goroutine runs when, allowing you to write concurrent code without manually managing threads.

The scheduler uses cooperative multitasking; goroutines yield control at certain points (e.g., during I/O or explicit runtime calls), ensuring that all goroutines get a chance to run. This model reduces the overhead and complexity associated with context switching in traditional threading models.

2.3. Communication with Channels

While our primary focus here is on goroutines, it's important to understand that channels are the idiomatic way to communicate between goroutines. Channels allow you to safely pass data from one goroutine to another without explicit locks.

2.3.1. Basic Channel Operations

Channels are declared using the chan keyword. You can send data into a channel using the <- operator, and receive data from a channel in a similar manner.

Example:

```go

ch := make(chan int)
go func() {
    ch <- 42  // Send 42 into the channel
```

```
} ()
value := <-ch  // Receive the value from the channel
fmt.Println(value)
```
Diagram Description:

Imagine two boxes labeled "Goroutine A" and "Goroutine B" connected by an arrow labeled "channel." One box sends data through the channel, and the other receives it, illustrating safe communication between concurrent tasks.

2.4. Benefits and Challenges of Concurrency

The benefits of using concurrency include increased efficiency, improved performance on multi-core systems, and a more responsive user experience. However, concurrency also introduces challenges such as race conditions, deadlocks, and the complexity of debugging concurrent code.

2.4.1. Race Conditions

A race condition occurs when two or more goroutines access the same variable concurrently and at least one of them modifies it. Go provides a race detector that can help identify these issues:

```bash
go run -race main.go
```
This command runs your program with the race detector enabled, alerting you to potential problems.

2.4.2. Deadlocks

A deadlock happens when goroutines wait indefinitely for each other to release resources or send/receive data. Understanding how to design your goroutine communication to avoid deadlocks is critical.

Real-World Analogy:

Imagine two people waiting for the other to speak in a conversation—nobody talks, and the conversation halts. Similarly, if two goroutines wait for each other's output without any progress, the program deadlocks.

2.5. The Go Memory Model and Concurrency

Go's memory model defines how goroutines interact with memory. It sets rules for how changes made by one goroutine become visible to another. Concepts such as atomic operations and mutexes (from the sync package) are sometimes necessary when you need fine-grained control over shared memory.

Understanding these details is essential for writing robust concurrent programs. However, many common patterns in Go (like using channels) abstract away much of the complexity, letting you focus on high-level design.

---

3. Tools and Setup

Before writing concurrent programs, it is important to ensure your development environment is properly configured. This section details the tools and setup procedures necessary for working with concurrency in Go.

3.1. Software Requirements

For this chapter, you'll need:

- **Go Compiler and Runtime:** Download from the official Go website.

- **IDE or Text Editor:** Visual Studio Code, GoLand, or Sublime Text, ideally with Go support.

- **Command-Line Interface:** Terminal on macOS/Linux or Command Prompt/PowerShell on Windows.

- **Version Control System:** Git for managing your code changes.

- **Race Detector:** Built into Go, so no extra installation is needed.

3.2. Setting Up Your IDE

Configuring your IDE correctly will improve your productivity when working with concurrent code. For example, if you use Visual Studio Code:

1. **Install VS Code:** Download and install it from code.visualstudio.com.

2. **Install the Go Extension:** Open the Extensions pane (Ctrl+Shift+X), search for "Go," and install the official extension.

3. **Configure Formatting:** Ensure that gofmt is enabled in your settings so that your code is automatically formatted.

4. **Set Up Debugging:** Configure the debugger to work with your Go projects for stepping through concurrent code.

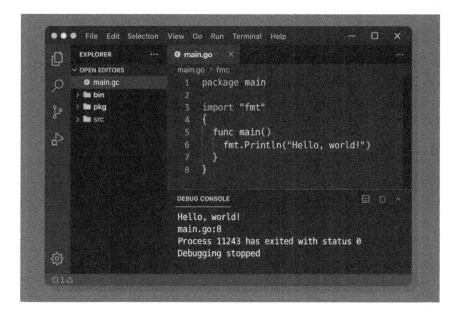

3.3. Command-Line Tools and Environment

Make sure that your terminal recognizes Go commands. Open your terminal and run:

bash

go version
A successful output confirms that Go is properly installed. Familiarize yourself with basic commands such as:

- **Running a Program:** go run main.go

- **Building an Executable:** go build

- **Running Tests with Race Detector:** go test -race ./...

3.4. Version Control and Project Organization

Use Git to manage your source code. In your project folder (e.g., go-concurrency-essentials), initialize a repository:

```bash
```

```
git init
git add .
git commit -m "Initial commit: Concurrency Essentials
chapter setup"
```
Organize your files into meaningful directories. For instance:

- **/cmd:** Contains the main executable(s).

- **/pkg:** Contains packages for concurrency utilities.

- **/test:** Contains test files for your concurrent functions.

4. Hands-on Examples & Projects

This section focuses on practical applications of concurrency using goroutines. We'll walk through several examples—from simple concurrent tasks to a complete project that demonstrates handling multiple operations simultaneously.

4.1. Starting Simple: A Basic Goroutine Example

Let's begin with a very simple example that shows how to launch a goroutine. The following program launches a goroutine that prints a message concurrently with the main function.

Example: Basic Goroutine

```go
go

package main

import (
    "fmt"
    "time"
)

func printMessage() {
    fmt.Println("Hello from the goroutine!")
}

func main() {
    go printMessage() // Start a new goroutine
    fmt.Println("Hello from the main function!")

    // Wait to ensure the goroutine completes before
program exit.
    time.Sleep(100 * time.Millisecond)
}
```

Explanation:

The go printMessage() statement starts a goroutine that runs concurrently with the main function. The call to time.Sleep ensures that the main function doesn't exit before the goroutine has a chance to execute.

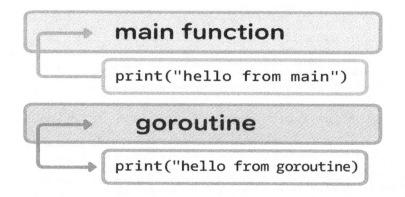

4.2. Concurrent Execution with Loops

Goroutines are especially useful in loops. Consider the following example where multiple goroutines are spawned within a loop to perform a task simultaneously.

Example: Loop with Goroutines

```go
package main

import (
    "fmt"
    "time"
)

func processTask(id int) {
    fmt.Printf("Task %d started\n", id)
    time.Sleep(50 * time.Millisecond)
    fmt.Printf("Task %d finished\n", id)
}

func main() {
    for i := 1; i <= 5; i++ {
        go processTask(i)
    }

    // Wait enough time for all tasks to finish.
    time.Sleep(300 * time.Millisecond)
}
```

Explanation:

This code spawns 5 goroutines, each processing a task. They run concurrently, and you see overlapping output as tasks start and finish. This demonstrates the power of goroutines to handle multiple operations simultaneously.

4.3. Handling Results: A Channel-Based Example

To coordinate and gather results from multiple goroutines, channels are used. The next example shows how to send data from goroutines back to the main function.

Example: Using Channels for Communication

```go
package main

import (
    "fmt"
    "time"
)

func processAndSend(id int, ch chan<- int) {
    time.Sleep(50 * time.Millisecond)
    ch <- id * id  // Send the square of the id
}

func main() {
    ch := make(chan int, 5)
    for i := 1; i <= 5; i++ {
        go processAndSend(i, ch)
    }

    // Collect results from the channel.
    for i := 1; i <= 5; i++ {
        result := <-ch
        fmt.Println("Received:", result)
    }
}
```

Explanation:

Each goroutine computes a value and sends it through a channel. The main function collects these values, demonstrating safe communication between concurrent tasks.

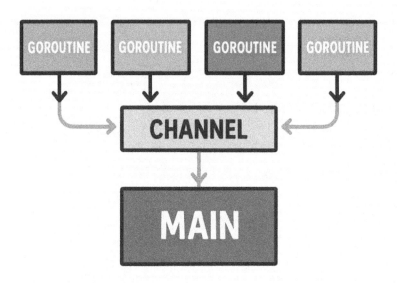

4.4. Short Project: A Program Handling Multiple Operations

Now let's build a short project that integrates the above examples into a cohesive command-line tool. This tool will simulate handling multiple operations concurrently. The program will:

1. Prompt the user for a list of numbers.

2. Launch a goroutine for each number to compute its square.

3. Collect and display the results concurrently.

Project Outline

Step 1: Read Input

Prompt the user to enter a list of space-separated integers.

Step 2: Launch Goroutines

For each integer, start a goroutine that calculates its square and sends the result via a channel.

Step 3: Collect and Display Results

The main function collects results from the channel and displays them.

Project Code: Concurrent Square Calculator

```go
package main

import (
    "bufio"
    "fmt"
    "os"
    "strconv"
    "strings"
    "time"
)

// square computes the square of a number and sends
it to the channel.
func square(num int, ch chan<- string) {
    time.Sleep(50 * time.Millisecond) // Simulate
some work
    result := num * num
    ch <- fmt.Sprintf("Square of %d is %d", num,
result)
}

func main() {
    reader := bufio.NewReader(os.Stdin)
```

```
fmt.Print("Enter integers separated by spaces: ")
input, _ := reader.ReadString('\n')
input = strings.TrimSpace(input)
numsStr := strings.Split(input, " ")

ch := make(chan string, len(numsStr))

// Start a goroutine for each number.
for _, s := range numsStr {
    num, err := strconv.Atoi(s)
    if err != nil {
        fmt.Printf("Invalid input '%s',
skipping.\n", s)
        continue
    }
    go square(num, ch)
}

// Collect and print results.
for i := 0; i < len(numsStr); i++ {
    fmt.Println(<-ch)
}
}
```

Explanation:

The program reads user input, splits it into individual numbers, and then launches a goroutine for each number to compute its square. A buffered channel collects the results, and the main function prints each result as it arrives.

4.5. Extending the Project

To deepen your understanding, consider extending the program:

- **Error Handling:**
  Improve input validation by reprompting the user on invalid input.

- **Additional Computations:**

  In addition to squaring numbers, compute other functions concurrently (e.g., cube, factorial).

- **Dynamic Operations:**

  Allow the user to choose which operation to perform on the input numbers.

Example Extension: Adding Operation Choice

```go
package main

import (
    "bufio"
    "fmt"
    "os"
    "strconv"
    "strings"
    "time"
)

func square(num int, ch chan<- string) {
    time.Sleep(50 * time.Millisecond)
    ch <- fmt.Sprintf("Square of %d is %d", num,
num*num)
}

func cube(num int, ch chan<- string) {
    time.Sleep(50 * time.Millisecond)
    ch <- fmt.Sprintf("Cube of %d is %d", num,
num*num*num)
}

func main() {
    reader := bufio.NewReader(os.Stdin)
    fmt.Print("Enter integers separated by spaces: ")
    input, _ := reader.ReadString('\n')
    input = strings.TrimSpace(input)
```

```go
    numsStr := strings.Split(input, " ")

    fmt.Print("Choose operation (1: Square, 2: Cube): ")
    opInput, _ := reader.ReadString('\n')
    opInput = strings.TrimSpace(opInput)

    ch := make(chan string, len(numsStr))
    for _, s := range numsStr {
        num, err := strconv.Atoi(s)
        if err != nil {
            fmt.Printf("Invalid input '%s', skipping.\n", s)
            continue
        }
        if opInput == "1" {
            go square(num, ch)
        } else if opInput == "2" {
            go cube(num, ch)
        } else {
            fmt.Println("Invalid operation selected.")
            return
        }
    }

    for i := 0; i < len(numsStr); i++ {
        fmt.Println(<-ch)
    }
}
```

Explanation:

This version lets the user select whether to compute the square or cube of each number. It demonstrates how adding simple control structures and additional goroutines can enhance your program's functionality.

5 . Conclusion & Next Steps

In this chapter, we've delved into the essentials of concurrency in Go—a critical skill for writing high-performance, responsive applications. We began with an introduction to key concepts like concurrency versus parallelism and explored the power of goroutines for lightweight, concurrent execution. We saw how channels enable safe communication between goroutines and learned how to coordinate multiple concurrent operations.

The hands-on examples gradually built up from simple goroutine launches to a full command-line tool that processes multiple operations simultaneously. Through these projects, you witnessed firsthand how Go's concurrency model allows you to harness the full power of modern hardware while keeping code simple and readable.

Advanced techniques such as worker pools, buffered channels, and synchronization with WaitGroups were introduced to help you optimize your concurrent programs further. Additionally, we discussed common pitfalls like race conditions and deadlocks, along with practical strategies for troubleshooting and debugging.

Looking ahead, here are some recommended next steps:

- **Deepen Your Understanding:**
  Experiment with more complex concurrency patterns, such as fan-in/fan-out, pipeline processing, and using the select statement for multiplexing channel operations.

- **Extend Your Projects:**

  Take the command-line tool you built and add features like dynamic task scheduling, timeout handling, or integration with external APIs.

- **Explore Advanced Libraries:**

  Consider using Go's concurrency utilities from the sync and context packages to manage cancellation, deadlines, and more complex workflows.

- **Benchmark and Profile:**

  Regularly benchmark your concurrent code to understand performance characteristics and use profiling tools like pprof to optimize bottlenecks.

- **Engage with the Community:**

  Read blogs, join forums, and contribute to open-source projects that use concurrency. Learning from real-world applications can provide invaluable insights.

Reflect on the importance of concurrency in building modern software. The ability to perform multiple tasks simultaneously not only improves performance but also makes your applications more responsive and scalable. By mastering these concepts, you are well on your way to developing robust systems that can handle the demands of today's multi-core environments.

Thank you for working through this chapter on concurrency essentials. The skills you've developed here—ranging from starting simple goroutines to orchestrating complex concurrent workflows—will be crucial as you build larger and more sophisticated applications. Continue to experiment, benchmark, and refine your concurrent programs, and explore how these techniques can be applied across different domains, from web servers to real-time data processing systems.

May your goroutines run smoothly, your channels flow without blockage, and your applications become ever more responsive and efficient. Happy coding, and best of luck as you advance further into the exciting world of concurrent programming with Go!

Chapter 8: Communication with Channels

1. Introduction

In today's fast-paced computing world, building software that can handle multiple tasks concurrently is crucial. Whether you're developing a web server that must manage dozens of client connections or a data processing pipeline that deals with real-time input, the ability to exchange data safely between concurrently executing parts of your program is key to building robust systems.

In Go, channels provide a safe and elegant way for goroutines to communicate. Unlike traditional shared-memory concurrency, where you must carefully synchronize access to variables, channels allow you to pass data between goroutines in a manner that is inherently safe. With channels, you can send and receive values with the guarantee that no two goroutines will corrupt each other's state—a critical advantage when designing concurrent systems.

This chapter begins with an overview of what channels are and why they're important. We'll define key terms such as "buffered" versus "unbuffered" channels, and explain concepts like blocking, synchronization, and data pipelining. We'll also discuss common pitfalls in concurrent programming and show you how to avoid them using channels. Throughout, you'll find real-world analogies—for example, comparing channels to postal mail systems, where letters (data) are safely delivered between senders and recipients.

After laying the theoretical groundwork, we'll walk through the tools and setup required to experiment with channels in Go. Whether you're using Visual Studio Code, GoLand, or another text editor, you'll learn how to configure your environment for efficient development and debugging of concurrent code.

The heart of the chapter is a hands-on project: building a server that handles concurrent requests. In this project, you will write a command-line server that listens for incoming connections and processes each request in a separate goroutine. You'll use channels to coordinate tasks, manage the flow of data, and even throttle the number of concurrent operations to avoid overloading the system. This example not only demonstrates the power of channels but also shows how to design systems that scale gracefully under load.

Throughout the chapter, our tone remains professional yet conversational. We explain technical concepts clearly while providing detailed code examples, complete with comments and step-by-step explanations. The material is structured to be accessible for beginners, while still offering insights that seasoned developers will appreciate. By the end of this chapter, you'll have a deep understanding of how channels work, how to avoid common concurrency pitfalls, and how to apply these concepts to build real-world applications.

Let's begin our journey by exploring the core theory behind channels and understanding why safe data exchange is critical for modern concurrent programming.

---

2. Core Concepts and Theory

2.1. Channels: A Concurrency Communication Primitive

Channels in Go are the primary mechanism for communication between goroutines. They enable data to flow safely from one goroutine to another, ensuring that concurrent operations do not interfere with each other. Channels work by providing a conduit through which data is sent and received; when one goroutine sends data to a channel, another goroutine can receive that data, and Go's runtime ensures that the exchange is synchronized.

2.1.1. Unbuffered vs. Buffered Channels

There are two primary types of channels in Go: unbuffered and buffered.

- **Unbuffered Channels:**
  An unbuffered channel does not have any capacity to store data. When a value is sent on an unbuffered channel, the sending goroutine is blocked until another goroutine receives from that channel. This makes unbuffered channels ideal for strict synchronization.

Example:

```go
ch := make(chan int) // Unbuffered channel
go func() {
    ch <- 42 // Send operation blocks until there is
a receiver.
}()
value := <-ch // Receives the value, unblocking the
sender.
fmt.Println(value) // Output: 42
```

- **Buffered Channels:**

  Buffered channels have a capacity, meaning they can hold a fixed number of values without blocking the sender. When a buffered channel is full, sending will block until some values are received.

Example:

```go
ch := make(chan int, 3) // Buffered channel with
capacity 3
ch <- 10 // Does not block (capacity not reached)
ch <- 20 // Does not block
ch <- 30 // Does not block
// Next send will block until a value is removed.
go func() {
    ch <- 40 // Will block until a receiver is ready.
}()
fmt.Println(<-ch) // Unblocks the sender.
```

Real-World Analogy:

Think of an unbuffered channel as a direct phone call—both parties must be available to communicate at the same time. A buffered channel is like a voicemail system where messages can be stored temporarily until the receiver is ready to listen.

2.1.2. Blocking Behavior and Synchronization

One of the most powerful aspects of channels is their ability to block a goroutine until a certain condition is met. When a goroutine attempts to send data on an unbuffered channel, it waits until another goroutine is ready to receive. Conversely, if a goroutine tries to receive from an empty channel, it blocks until data is available. This built-in synchronization mechanism greatly simplifies concurrent programming by removing the need for explicit locks.

2.1.3. Directional Channels

Channels can also be restricted to only sending or receiving data, which can make your code safer and more self-documenting. For example, you can declare a channel parameter that is "send-only" or "receive-only" within a function.

Example:

```go
func sendData(ch chan<- int, data int) {
    ch <- data
}

func receiveData(ch <-chan int) int {
    return <-ch
}
```

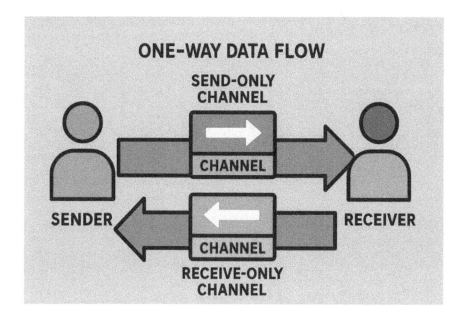

2.2. Safe Data Exchange: Why Channels Matter

Channels not only facilitate communication but also ensure that data exchange between goroutines is done safely. This prevents race conditions—a situation where multiple goroutines access shared data simultaneously, leading to unpredictable behavior.

2.2.1. Eliminating Race Conditions

Race conditions occur when two or more goroutines try to read and write the same data without proper synchronization. By using channels, you can structure your code so that only one goroutine interacts with a piece of data at a time, thereby eliminating many common concurrency issues.

Example:

```go
go

var counter int = 0
ch := make(chan int)

// Goroutine that increments the counter.
go func() {
    for i := 0; i < 100; i++ {
        counter++ // This could cause a race
condition.
        ch <- counter
    }
}()

// Main function receiving values.
for i := 0; i < 100; i++ {
    fmt.Println(<-ch)
}
```

Explanation:

While the above code might seem simple, it risks a race condition on the counter variable if multiple goroutines attempted to update it simultaneously. Channels can be used to ensure that such modifications are coordinated, or alternatively, synchronization primitives (like mutexes) may be employed. In practice, channels allow you to structure programs that minimize shared state.

2.3. The Role of Channels in Concurrency Patterns

Channels are not only useful for basic communication; they are central to many concurrency patterns that solve common problems. Some popular patterns include:

- **Pipeline Pattern:**

  Data flows through a series of stages, with each stage running concurrently. Channels pass data from one stage to the next.

- **Fan-In/Fan-Out Pattern:**

  Multiple goroutines send data into a single channel (fan-in) or a single goroutine distributes work to multiple goroutines (fan-out). This is useful for parallel processing and load balancing.

- **Worker Pools:**

  A fixed number of worker goroutines process tasks from a shared channel. This pattern helps control concurrency and manage system resources efficiently.

Real-World Analogy:

Imagine an assembly line in a factory. Each station (goroutine) performs a specific task and passes the item (data) along a conveyor belt (channel). By organizing the work this way, the assembly line operates efficiently without bottlenecks.

2.4. Common Pitfalls with Channels and How to Avoid Them

Even though channels simplify concurrent programming, there are still pitfalls you must avoid:

2.4.1. Deadlocks

A deadlock occurs when goroutines are stuck waiting for each other indefinitely. A typical scenario involves sending to an unbuffered channel when no goroutine is receiving, or vice versa.

Example of Deadlock:

```go
ch := make(chan int)
ch <- 5 // This send blocks indefinitely since no
goroutine is receiving.
```
Solution:

Ensure that every channel send has a corresponding receive. Use buffered channels if necessary or structure your goroutines so that blocking operations are minimized.

2.4.2. Unintended Blocking

Sometimes, a goroutine may block unexpectedly if the channel is not used correctly. For instance, reading from an empty channel without a timeout or select statement can cause your program to hang.

Tip:

Use the select statement with a default case to prevent indefinite blocking:

```go
select {
case data := <-ch:
    fmt.Println("Received:", data)
default:
    fmt.Println("No data available")
}
```

2.4.3. Channel Leaks

A channel leak happens when goroutines are left waiting on a channel that will never be closed. This can occur if your program logic fails to close channels when they are no longer needed.

Best Practice:
Always close channels when no further values will be sent:

```go
close(ch)
```
Ensure that receivers check for the channel's closure to terminate loops gracefully.

---

3. Tools and Setup

Before you start experimenting with channels in your code, it's important to have your development environment properly configured. This section covers the tools and setup procedures necessary to work with channels in Go.

3.1. Required Software

For this chapter, you need:

- **Go Compiler and Runtime:** Download from the official Go website.

- **Integrated Development Environment (IDE) or Code Editor:** Popular choices include Visual Studio Code, GoLand, or Sublime Text with Go support.

- **Command-Line Interface:** Terminal on macOS/Linux or Command Prompt/PowerShell on Windows.

- **Version Control System:** Git is highly recommended for managing your code.

- **Race Detector:** Go's built-in race detector is useful for debugging concurrent programs.

3.2. Installing and Configuring Your Editor

For optimal productivity, configure your IDE to support Go's concurrency features:

1. **Install Your Editor:** For example, download and install Visual Studio Code.

2. **Add the Go Extension:** Open the Extensions pane (Ctrl+Shift+X), search for "Go," and install the official extension.

3. **Enable Code Formatting:** Ensure gofmt is set to format your code automatically.

4. **Configure Debugging:** Set up your debugging environment to step through concurrent code—this may involve setting breakpoints and examining channel states.

5.   **Workspace Organization:** Create a dedicated workspace for concurrency projects (e.g., a folder named go-channels).

3.3. Command-Line Setup

Ensure that your terminal is correctly configured to run Go commands. Open your terminal and type:

```bash
go version
```

If you see the Go version printed, your installation is correct. Familiarize yourself with commands such as:

- **Running a Program:** go run main.go

- **Building Executables:** go build

- **Testing with Race Detector:** go test -race ./...

3.4. Version Control and Project Structure

Using Git to manage your source code is a best practice, especially when working on complex projects. In your project folder (e.g., go-channels), initialize a repository:

```bash
git init
git add .
git commit -m "Initial commit: Channel communication
examples"
```

Organize your project with a clear directory structure:

- **/cmd:** Contains the main executables.

- **/pkg:** Contains reusable packages, including your channel communication utilities.

- **/test:** Contains test files for your concurrent code.

Diagram Description:
Visualize a directory tree with folders such as "cmd," "pkg," and "test," each containing relevant source files. This organization is critical as your project scales.

---

4. Hands-on Examples & Projects

This section is devoted to practical, hands-on examples that demonstrate how to use channels effectively. We'll start with simple examples to illustrate basic channel operations, then work up to a more complex project: building a server that manages concurrent requests.

4.1. Basic Channel Operations

Let's begin with a simple example that demonstrates creating a channel, sending a value into it, and receiving that value.

Example: Simple Channel Communication

```go
package main

import (
    "fmt"
)

func main() {
```

```
// Create an unbuffered channel of type int.
ch := make(chan int)

// Launch a goroutine that sends a value.
go func() {
    ch <- 42
}()

// Receive the value from the channel.
value := <-ch
fmt.Println("Received value:", value)
}
```

Explanation:

This program creates an unbuffered channel, sends the integer 42 from a goroutine, and receives it in the main function. Notice how the send operation blocks until the main function receives the value.

4.2. Buffered Channels: Enhancing Throughput

Buffered channels allow you to send multiple values without waiting for an immediate receiver. They are especially useful when you expect bursts of data.

Example: Buffered Channel Usage

```go
package main

import (
    "fmt"
)

func main() {
    // Create a buffered channel with capacity 3.
    ch := make(chan string, 3)
```

```go
    // Send three values without blocking.
    ch <- "first"
    ch <- "second"
    ch <- "third"

    // Now receive the values.
    fmt.Println(<-ch)
    fmt.Println(<-ch)
    fmt.Println(<-ch)
}
```

Explanation:

This example shows that you can send three values to a buffered channel without blocking. Once the channel is full, further sends would block until a receiver removes some values.

4.3. Advanced Channel Techniques: Select and Timeouts

The select statement is a powerful tool that lets you wait on multiple channel operations simultaneously. It can be used to implement timeouts or prioritize certain operations.

Example: Using Select with Timeout

```go
go

package main

import (
    "fmt"
    "time"
)

func main() {
    ch := make(chan int)

    go func() {
        time.Sleep(100 * time.Millisecond)
```

```
        ch <- 10
    }()

    select {
    case val := <-ch:
        fmt.Println("Received:", val)
    case <-time.After(50 * time.Millisecond):
        fmt.Println("Timeout: No value received in
time.")
    }
}
```

Explanation:

This program launches a goroutine that sends a value after 100 milliseconds. The select statement waits for the value, but if 50 milliseconds pass without receiving data, the timeout case is executed.

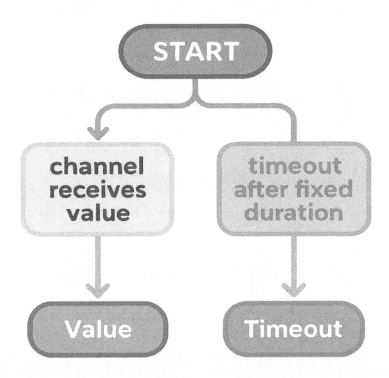

4.4. Hands-on Project: Building a Concurrent Server

Now, let's put everything together with a hands-on project—a simple server that manages concurrent requests using channels. In this project, we will build a command-line server that listens for simulated client requests, processes them concurrently using goroutines, and communicates the results back to the main thread via channels.

Project Overview

Objective:
Create a server that handles multiple operations concurrently, demonstrating safe communication with channels.

Features:

- Simulate incoming client requests.

- Process each request in a separate goroutine.

- Use channels to collect and aggregate responses.

- Gracefully shut down the server when all requests are handled.

Design:

- A main server loop that listens for requests.

- A worker function that processes requests.

- A channel that carries the results of processing.

Step 1: Define the Request and Response Structures

Create a file named server.go and define the data structures:

```go
package main

import "fmt"

// Request represents a client request.
type Request struct {
    ID      int
    Payload string
}

// Response represents the server's response.
type Response struct {
    RequestID int
    Result    string
}
```

Step 2: Write the Worker Function

The worker function processes each request and sends a response via a channel:

```go
func processRequest(req Request, resCh chan<-
Response) {
    // Simulate processing time.
    // In a real server, this would be some
meaningful work.
    result := fmt.Sprintf("Processed payload '%s' for
request %d", req.Payload, req.ID)
    resCh <- Response{RequestID: req.ID, Result:
result}
}
```

Step 3: Build the Main Server Loop

The main function will simulate receiving client requests, launching a goroutine for each request, and collecting responses:

```go
package main

import (
    "fmt"
    "math/rand"
    "time"
)

func main() {
    // Seed the random number generator.
    rand.Seed(time.Now().UnixNano())

    // Create a channel for responses.
    resCh := make(chan Response, 10)

    // Simulate incoming requests.
    requests := []Request{
        {ID: 1, Payload: "data1"},
        {ID: 2, Payload: "data2"},
        {ID: 3, Payload: "data3"},
        {ID: 4, Payload: "data4"},
        {ID: 5, Payload: "data5"},
    }

    fmt.Println("Server: Received requests.
Processing concurrently...")

    // Launch a goroutine for each request.
    for _, req := range requests {
        go processRequest(req, resCh)
    }

    // Collect responses.
    for i := 0; i < len(requests); i++ {
        res := <-resCh
```

```
        fmt.Printf("Server: Response for request %d -
%s\n", res.RequestID, res.Result)
    }

    fmt.Println("Server: All requests processed.
Shutting down.")
}
```

Explanation:

The main function seeds the random generator (simulating unpredictable processing times), creates a buffered channel for responses, and defines a list of sample requests. It then launches a goroutine for each request, collects the responses, and prints them. This project demonstrates safe data exchange between concurrently executing goroutines using channels.

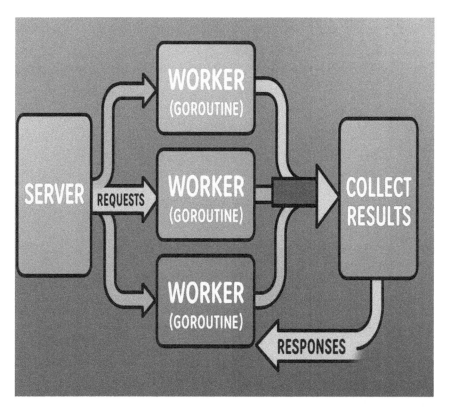

4.5. Enhancing the Server with Additional Features

To further solidify your understanding, consider these enhancements:

- **Dynamic Request Generation:**
  Instead of a fixed list, generate random requests continuously until a termination signal is received.

- **Timeout Handling:**
  Use the select statement to implement timeouts when waiting for responses, ensuring the server doesn't hang if a request fails.

- **Graceful Shutdown:**
  Implement a mechanism to close the channel and terminate the server once all active goroutines have finished processing.

Example Enhancement: Dynamic Request Simulation with Timeout

```go
package main

import (
    "fmt"
    "math/rand"
    "time"
)

func main() {
    rand.Seed(time.Now().UnixNano())
    resCh := make(chan Response, 10)

    // Simulate dynamic request generation.
    go func() {
        for i := 1; i <= 10; i++ {
```

```
        req := Request{ID: i, Payload:
fmt.Sprintf("data%d", i)}
            go processRequest(req, resCh)
            time.Sleep(time.Duration(rand.Intn(100))
* time.Millisecond)
        }
        close(resCh)
    }()

    // Process responses with timeout.
    for res := range resCh {
        fmt.Printf("Received response for request %d:
%s\n", res.RequestID, res.Result)
    }

    fmt.Println("Server: All dynamic requests
processed. Shutting down.")
}
```

Explanation:

This version runs a goroutine that continuously generates requests and
eventually closes the response channel. The main loop uses a range over
the channel, gracefully terminating when all responses have been received.

---

5 . Conclusion & Next Steps

In this chapter, we have explored the fundamentals and advanced
techniques of communication with channels in Go. We began by
understanding the core concept of channels—how they allow safe data
exchange between goroutines and enable synchronization without explicit
locks. We defined unbuffered versus buffered channels, discussed
blocking behavior, and introduced techniques to avoid common pitfalls
such as deadlocks, unintended blocking, and channel leaks.

Our discussion moved from theory to practical application, with numerous code examples demonstrating how to create, send, receive, and multiplex data using channels. We explored the use of the select statement for handling multiple channel operations concurrently, and looked at strategies for optimizing channel throughput. In the hands-on section, you built a concurrent server—a real-world project that simulates handling multiple client requests simultaneously. This project demonstrated how to use channels to coordinate goroutines effectively, ensuring that data is processed in a safe and organized manner.

As you continue to work with Go, remember that channels are more than just a tool—they are a powerful abstraction that can help you write elegant, robust, and efficient concurrent programs. The techniques discussed here form the basis for many advanced concurrency patterns. Next steps in your learning journey might include:

- **Experimentation:**
  Modify the server project by adding features such as dynamic request generation, improved error handling, or integrating a graceful shutdown mechanism.

- **Advanced Concurrency Patterns:**
  Explore patterns like fan-in/fan-out, pipelines, and worker pools to manage large-scale concurrent workloads.

- **Profiling and Benchmarking:**
  Use Go's profiling tools to analyze the performance of your concurrent applications and identify areas for optimization.

- **Community Resources:**

  Engage with online communities, read Go blogs, and study open-source projects that make heavy use of channels. Sharing experiences and solutions will further refine your understanding.

- **Integrating with Other Concurrency Primitives:**

  Learn about synchronization techniques such as mutexes and condition variables from the sync package, and how they complement channels when dealing with shared state.

Reflect on the importance of safe communication in concurrent programming. The principles of channel-based communication not only reduce complexity but also prevent many of the pitfalls associated with traditional multithreading. By mastering channels, you empower your applications to scale and perform reliably under load.

Thank you for exploring this chapter on communication with channels. The skills you've developed here are foundational to building concurrent applications that make full use of modern multi-core architectures. Continue to experiment, build new projects, and explore advanced topics in Go concurrency. Your journey into writing robust, high-performance concurrent code is just beginning.

May your channels be buffered when needed, your goroutines synchronized perfectly, and your concurrent programs run smoothly and efficiently. Happy coding, and best of luck as you apply these techniques to your own projects!

Chapter 9: Error Handling and Testing

---

1. Introduction

Error handling and testing are critical components of software development that ensure applications behave reliably, even in the face of unexpected conditions. In a language like Go, error handling is explicit and straightforward, requiring developers to check and respond to errors at every stage of their program. Testing, on the other hand, verifies that code behaves as expected and helps catch issues before they reach production.

When you build applications, you inevitably face situations where things don't go as planned. An API might receive malformed requests, a file may be missing, or a network call might fail. Instead of letting these issues crash your application or, worse, leave it in an unpredictable state, Go encourages you to handle errors gracefully. By doing so, you can provide meaningful feedback, log useful information, and maintain control over your program's execution.

In this chapter, we start by exploring key concepts in error handling. We discuss how errors are represented in Go, why explicit error checking is preferred over exceptions in some cases, and how to propagate errors to higher levels of the application. You will learn the idiomatic approach to handling errors using simple if-statements and helper functions. We'll also examine how to create custom error types that provide additional context, making debugging easier.

Next, we introduce testing frameworks and techniques in Go. Testing isn't just about verifying that your code works—it's also about documenting its behavior and protecting against regressions as your codebase evolves. We'll look at Go's built-in testing package, how to write unit tests, and how to organize your tests for clarity and efficiency. You will see examples of table-driven tests, which allow you to run multiple scenarios through the same test function. We'll also discuss best practices for writing clean, maintainable tests that mirror real-world usage.

The chapter is structured to gradually build your understanding. First, we cover the theory behind error handling and testing, complete with real-world analogies and code examples that break down complex ideas into manageable pieces. Next, we describe the tools and environment setup necessary for developing and testing Go code. Finally, the heart of the chapter is a hands-on project where you develop a small API. This API is designed with comprehensive tests for each endpoint, giving you a practical example of how error handling and testing integrate into the development process.

Throughout the chapter, our approach is clear and methodical. We define key terms as they appear, use analogies to simplify difficult concepts, and provide code examples that are cleanly formatted and extensively commented. Whether you're new to Go or an experienced developer refining your craft, the lessons here will help you build robust and resilient applications.

By the end of this chapter, you will be able to:

- Capture and handle errors gracefully in your Go programs.

- Create custom error types that add context to error messages.

- Write effective tests using Go's testing framework.

- Develop a small API and write comprehensive tests for each of its endpoints.

- Understand the best practices in error handling and testing that contribute to the overall reliability and maintainability of your code.

Let's now explore the core concepts behind error handling and testing in Go.

2. Core Concepts and Theory

2.1. Error Handling in Go

Go's error handling philosophy is built around the concept that errors are just values. Rather than using exceptions, Go functions return an error as a second value (or part of multiple return values), which callers can inspect and handle accordingly.

2.1.1. The Built-in Error Interface

At the heart of Go's error handling is the built-in error interface:

```go
type error interface {
    Error() string
}
```

Any type that implements this method satisfies the error interface. This design means you can create custom error types to carry more context about the error situation.

Example:

```go
package main

import (
    "errors"
    "fmt"
)

func main() {
    err := errors.New("something went wrong")
    if err != nil {
        fmt.Println("Error:", err.Error())
    }
}
```

In this simple example, we use the errors.New function to create a new error. The error's message is then printed if an error occurred.

2.1.2. Propagating Errors

When a function encounters an error, it should return that error to its caller, allowing the caller to decide how to handle it. This explicit error propagation makes it clear where errors occur and how they should be handled.

Example:

```go
func readData(filename string) (string, error) {
    // Imagine some file reading logic here.
    return "", errors.New("file not found")
}

func main() {
    data, err := readData("config.txt")
    if err != nil {
        fmt.Println("Failed to read data:", err)
        return
    }
    fmt.Println("Data:", data)
}
```

Here, the readData function returns an error if the file is not found. The caller checks the error and handles it accordingly.

2.1.3. Custom Error Types

Sometimes, the standard error isn't enough. You may want to include additional context about the error. Custom error types let you do this.

Example:

```go
package main

import (
    "fmt"
)

type ValidationError struct {
    Field    string
```

```
    Message string
}

func (v ValidationError) Error() string {
    return fmt.Sprintf("Validation failed for %s:
%s", v.Field, v.Message)
}

func validateInput(input string) error {
    if input == "" {
        return ValidationError{"input", "cannot be
empty"}
    }
    return nil
}

func main() {
    err := validateInput("")
    if err != nil {
        fmt.Println("Error:", err)
    }
}
```

This custom error type, ValidationError, provides specific details about the error, which is helpful for debugging and logging.

2.2. Testing in Go

Testing is an essential aspect of ensuring that your code behaves as expected. Go provides a robust testing framework as part of its standard library, making it easy to write, run, and manage tests.

2.2.1. The Testing Package

The testing package in Go allows you to write unit tests by creating functions with the prefix Test that take a *testing.T parameter.

Example:

```go
go
```

```
package main

import "testing"

func add(a, b int) int {
    return a + b
}

func TestAdd(t *testing.T) {
    expected := 5
    if result := add(2, 3); result != expected {
        t.Errorf("add(2, 3) = %d; want %d", result,
expected)
    }
}
```

This example demonstrates a simple test for an add function. The test compares the actual output with the expected output and reports an error if they do not match.

2.2.2. Table-Driven Tests

A common pattern in Go is table-driven tests, where multiple test cases are defined in a slice and iterated over within a single test function. This approach makes tests concise and easy to extend.

Example:

```
go

func TestAddTable(t *testing.T) {
    tests := []struct {
        a, b, expected int
    }{
        {2, 3, 5},
        {5, 7, 12},
        {-1, 1, 0},
    }

    for _, tt := range tests {
```

```
    result := add(tt.a, tt.b)
    if result != tt.expected {
        t.Errorf("add(%d, %d) = %d; want %d",
tt.a, tt.b, result, tt.expected)
        }
    }
}
```

This test function defines multiple scenarios and ensures that the add function works correctly in each case.

2.3. Error Handling Best Practices

When handling errors, aim for clarity and consistency. Some best practices include:

- **Check errors immediately:** Handle an error as soon as it is returned.

- **Wrap errors for context:** Use custom error types or the fmt.Errorf function with %w to wrap errors with additional context.

- **Return errors to callers:** Avoid swallowing errors silently; let higher-level functions decide how to handle them.

- **Document error behavior:** Clearly state what errors a function might return in its documentation.

Real-World Analogy:

Imagine a factory assembly line where each station inspects its product and flags defects immediately. This way, issues can be fixed at the earliest opportunity rather than causing a complete shutdown later on.

2.4. Testing Strategies

Effective testing requires more than just writing tests. It's about structuring your tests to cover a wide range of scenarios and ensuring that your tests are maintainable over time.

2.4.1. Unit Testing

Unit tests focus on testing individual functions or methods. They should be fast, independent, and cover both typical and edge-case scenarios.

2.4.2. Integration Testing

Integration tests validate the interactions between multiple components. For instance, testing an API endpoint might involve checking that various layers of your application work together as expected.

2.4.3. Test Coverage

Aim for high test coverage, but focus on meaningful tests rather than just hitting a percentage target. Use Go's built-in tools to measure coverage:

```bash
go test -cover
```

2.4.4. Continuous Integration

Integrate testing into your development workflow using CI/CD pipelines. Automate your tests to run on every commit, ensuring that regressions are caught early.

3. Tools and Setup

Before writing error handling and tests for your API project, you must ensure your development environment is correctly set up.

3.1. Software Requirements

For this chapter, you need:

- **Go Compiler and Runtime:** Available from the official Go website.

- **IDE or Code Editor:** Recommended options include Visual Studio Code, GoLand, or Sublime Text with Go support.

- **Command-Line Interface:** Terminal on macOS/Linux or Command Prompt/PowerShell on Windows.

- **Version Control System:** Git for managing your code changes.

- **Testing Tools:** The go test command and optionally third-party libraries such as testify for more expressive assertions.

3.2. Configuring Your IDE for Testing

In Visual Studio Code, install the Go extension to enable features such as:

- Syntax highlighting for test files.

- Code formatting via gofmt.

- Integrated terminal support to run go test.

- Debugging support for tests.

3.3. Command-Line Setup

Verify that Go is installed by running:

```bash

go version
```
Familiarize yourself with commands such as:

- **Run Tests:** go test ./...

- **Test with Coverage:** go test -cover ./...

- **Verbose Output:** go test -v ./...

3.4. Version Control and Project Structure

Set up your project directory for the API project:

- **/cmd:** Contains the main executable (e.g., main.go).

- **/pkg/api:** Contains the API implementation.

- **/test:** Contains your test files.

- **/docs:** (Optional) Documentation and API design notes.

Initialize your Git repository:

```bash

git init
git add .
git commit -m "Initial commit: API project setup with error handling and tests"
```
Organize your files to separate production code from tests, ensuring a

clear structure.

4. Hands-on Examples & Projects

In this section, we build a practical project—a small API with comprehensive tests for each endpoint. This project demonstrates error handling and testing in a real-world context.

4.1. Project Overview: Small API

Our API will simulate a simple data store where clients can:

- Retrieve a list of items.

- Add a new item.

- Update an existing item.

- Delete an item.

We will handle errors gracefully (e.g., invalid input, item not found) and write tests to cover each endpoint.

4.2. Defining the API Structure

Start by designing your API. In the /pkg/api folder, create a file api.go that defines the core structures and functions.

Example: API Data Structures and Functions

```go
package api

import (
```

```go
    "errors"
    "sync"
)

// Item represents a single resource in the API.
type Item struct {
    ID     int
    Name   string
    Value  string
}

// API represents our simple API server.
type API struct {
    mu     sync.RWMutex
    items  map[int]Item
    nextID int
}

// NewAPI initializes a new API instance.
func NewAPI() *API {
    return &API{
        items:  make(map[int]Item),
        nextID: 1,
    }
}

// GetItems returns a slice of all items.
func (a *API) GetItems() []Item {
    a.mu.RLock()
    defer a.mu.RUnlock()

    result := make([]Item, 0, len(a.items))
    for _, item := range a.items {
        result = append(result, item)
    }
    return result
}

// AddItem adds a new item and returns the created
item.
func (a *API) AddItem(name, value string) Item {
    a.mu.Lock()
    defer a.mu.Unlock()
```

```go
    item := Item{
        ID:     a.nextID,
        Name:   name,
        Value:  value,
    }
    a.items[a.nextID] = item
    a.nextID++
    return item
}

// UpdateItem updates an existing item.
func (a *API) UpdateItem(id int, name, value string)
(Item, error) {
    a.mu.Lock()
    defer a.mu.Unlock()

    item, exists := a.items[id]
    if !exists {
        return Item{}, errors.New("item not found")
    }
    item.Name = name
    item.Value = value
    a.items[id] = item
    return item, nil
}

// DeleteItem removes an item by ID.
func (a *API) DeleteItem(id int) error {
    a.mu.Lock()
    defer a.mu.Unlock()

    if _, exists := a.items[id]; !exists {
        return errors.New("item not found")
    }
    delete(a.items, id)
    return nil
}
```

Explanation:

This code defines an API that uses a map to store items and a read-write

mutex for concurrent access. Functions for retrieving, adding, updating, and deleting items handle errors by returning descriptive messages when operations fail.

4.3. Creating the HTTP Server

In the /cmd folder, create main.go to expose the API via HTTP endpoints using the standard net/http package.

Example: HTTP Server Implementation

```go
package main

import (
    "encoding/json"
    "log"
    "net/http"
    "strconv"

    "your_project_path/pkg/api"
)

var apiServer = api.NewAPI()

func getItemsHandler(w http.ResponseWriter, r
*http.Request) {
    items := apiServer.GetItems()
    json.NewEncoder(w).Encode(items)
}

func addItemHandler(w http.ResponseWriter, r
*http.Request) {
    var input struct {
        Name  string `json:"name"`
        Value string `json:"value"`
    }
    if err := json.NewDecoder(r.Body).Decode(&input);
err != nil {
        http.Error(w, "Invalid input",
http.StatusBadRequest)
```

```go
        return
    }
    item := apiServer.AddItem(input.Name,
input.Value)
    w.WriteHeader(http.StatusCreated)
    json.NewEncoder(w).Encode(item)
}

func updateItemHandler(w http.ResponseWriter, r
*http.Request) {
    idStr := r.URL.Query().Get("id")
    id, err := strconv.Atoi(idStr)
    if err != nil {
        http.Error(w, "Invalid ID",
http.StatusBadRequest)
        return
    }
    var input struct {
        Name  string `json:"name"`
        Value string `json:"value"`
    }
    if err := json.NewDecoder(r.Body).Decode(&input);
err != nil {
        http.Error(w, "Invalid input",
http.StatusBadRequest)
        return
    }
    updatedItem, err := apiServer.UpdateItem(id,
input.Name, input.Value)
    if err != nil {
        http.Error(w, err.Error(),
http.StatusNotFound)
        return
    }
    json.NewEncoder(w).Encode(updatedItem)
}

func deleteItemHandler(w http.ResponseWriter, r
*http.Request) {
    idStr := r.URL.Query().Get("id")
    id, err := strconv.Atoi(idStr)
    if err != nil {
        http.Error(w, "Invalid ID",
http.StatusBadRequest)
```

```
        return
    }
    if err := apiServer.DeleteItem(id); err != nil {
        http.Error(w, err.Error(),
http.StatusNotFound)
        return
    }
    w.WriteHeader(http.StatusNoContent)
}

func main() {
    http.HandleFunc("/items", func(w
http.ResponseWriter, r *http.Request) {
        switch r.Method {
        case http.MethodGet:
            getItemsHandler(w, r)
        case http.MethodPost:
            addItemHandler(w, r)
        case http.MethodPut:
            updateItemHandler(w, r)
        case http.MethodDelete:
            deleteItemHandler(w, r)
        default:
            http.Error(w, "Method not allowed",
http.StatusMethodNotAllowed)
        }
    })

    log.Println("API server is running on port
8080...")
    log.Fatal(http.ListenAndServe(":8080", nil))
}
```

Explanation:

The HTTP server defines endpoints to interact with our API. Each endpoint handles errors gracefully—returning appropriate HTTP status codes and error messages when input is invalid or operations fail.

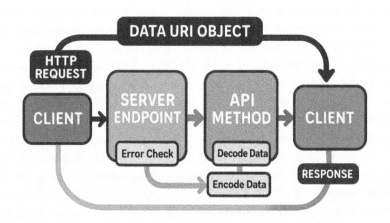

4.4. Writing Comprehensive Tests for the API

Now, let's write tests for each endpoint. Create a file api_test.go in the /test directory.

Example: API Endpoint Tests

```go
package api_test

import (
    "bytes"
    "encoding/json"
    "io/ioutil"
    "net/http"
    "net/http/httptest"
    "strconv"
    "testing"

    "your_project_path/pkg/api"
    "your_project_path/cmd"
```

```
)

func TestAddItemHandler(t *testing.T) {
    payload := []byte(`{"name": "TestItem", "value":
"TestValue"}`)
    req, err := http.NewRequest("POST", "/items",
bytes.NewBuffer(payload))
    if err != nil {
        t.Fatal(err)
    }
    rr := httptest.NewRecorder()
    handler := http.HandlerFunc(cmd.AddItemHandler)

    handler.ServeHTTP(rr, req)

    if status := rr.Code; status !=
http.StatusCreated {
        t.Errorf("handler returned wrong status code:
got %v want %v", status, http.StatusCreated)
    }

    var item api.Item
    if err := json.Unmarshal(rr.Body.Bytes(), &item);
err != nil {
        t.Fatal(err)
    }

    if item.Name != "TestItem" {
        t.Errorf("Expected item name 'TestItem', got
'%s'", item.Name)
    }
}

func TestGetItemsHandler(t *testing.T) {
    // First, add an item.
    payload := []byte(`{"name": "TestItem2", "value":
"TestValue2"}`)
    req, err := http.NewRequest("POST", "/items",
bytes.NewBuffer(payload))
    if err != nil {
        t.Fatal(err)
    }
    rr := httptest.NewRecorder()
    cmd.AddItemHandler(rr, req)
```

```go
    // Now, retrieve items.
    req, err = http.NewRequest("GET", "/items", nil)
    if err != nil {
        t.Fatal(err)
    }
    rr = httptest.NewRecorder()
    handler := http.HandlerFunc(cmd.GetItemsHandler)
    handler.ServeHTTP(rr, req)

    if status := rr.Code; status != http.StatusOK {
        t.Errorf("handler returned wrong status code:
got %v want %v", status, http.StatusOK)
    }

    var items []api.Item
    body, _ := ioutil.ReadAll(rr.Body)
    if err := json.Unmarshal(body, &items); err !=
nil {
        t.Fatal(err)
    }

    if len(items) == 0 {
        t.Error("Expected at least one item, got
zero")
    }
}

// Similar tests can be written for update and delete
handlers.
```

Explanation:

These tests simulate HTTP requests to our API endpoints and verify that the responses match expectations. By using the httptest package, we can test our API in isolation from an actual server.

4.5. Running the Tests

Run your tests using:

```bash
```

```
go test -v ./test
```

The verbose flag ensures that you see detailed output, which is useful for diagnosing issues.

4.6. Visualizing Test Coverage

You can also generate test coverage reports:

```bash
```

```
go test -coverprofile=coverage.out ./test && go tool
cover -html=coverage.out
```

This command produces an HTML report showing which parts of your code are covered by tests, highlighting areas that might need more testing.

5 . Conclusion & Next Steps

In this chapter, we have delved into the fundamentals and advanced techniques of error handling and testing in Go. We began by exploring how Go treats errors as values, emphasizing the importance of explicit error checking and propagation. You learned to create custom error types that add context to error messages and discovered best practices for handling errors gracefully. This approach ensures that your applications remain robust and that issues are surfaced early in the execution flow.

We then shifted our focus to testing—an indispensable part of any software development process. Through examples of unit tests, table-driven tests, and integration tests, you learned how to verify your code's behavior and guard against regressions. Our discussion on continuous integration highlighted the value of automating your tests to maintain high code quality over time.

The hands-on project—developing a small API with comprehensive tests for each endpoint—served as a practical demonstration of these principles. By designing endpoints that handle errors gracefully and writing tests that validate every scenario, you now have a clear roadmap for building resilient APIs. This project not only reinforces the theory but also provides you with a solid template that can be extended for more complex applications.

Looking ahead, your next steps might include:

- **Extending the API:**
  Add more endpoints, improve error messages, and handle additional edge cases.

- **Adopting Test-Driven Development:**
  Write tests before implementing features to drive design decisions and ensure comprehensive coverage.

- **Exploring Advanced Testing Tools:**
  Consider integrating third-party testing libraries like testify for more expressive assertions and better organization.

- **Integrating with CI/CD Pipelines:**
  Automate your testing process using tools like GitHub Actions, Travis CI, or CircleCI to ensure that every commit is validated.

- **Refining Error Handling:**

  Experiment with error wrapping, structured logging, and context propagation to build even more robust applications.

Reflect on how the careful handling of errors and rigorous testing contribute to the overall quality and maintainability of your code. In a production environment, users will rarely see the inner workings of your error handling logic, but they will benefit from its reliability and robustness. The discipline of testing, meanwhile, ensures that your code remains functional and that new changes do not inadvertently break existing functionality.

Thank you for working through this chapter on error handling and testing. The techniques and practices you've learned here are fundamental to writing professional, high-quality software. Continue to build on these skills as you explore more advanced topics and larger projects in Go. Your commitment to robust error handling and comprehensive testing will serve you well throughout your programming career.

May your errors be handled gracefully, your tests catch every edge case, and your applications remain resilient and reliable. Happy coding, and best of luck as you apply these principles to your own projects!

Chapter 10: Organizing Code for Scalability

1. Introduction

In modern software development, scalability is not merely about handling increased load—it's also about organizing your code in a way that makes it easier to maintain, extend, and debug over time. As projects grow, the structure of your codebase becomes critically important. Without a clear and modular organization, even a well-functioning program can become a tangled mess, slowing development and making future enhancements a daunting challenge.

In this chapter, we explore best practices for structuring your Go projects and packages for scalability. You will learn how to split a monolithic codebase into well-organized modules, design packages that are reusable and maintainable, and adopt patterns that promote clarity and simplicity. Whether you're a beginner just starting out, a professional developer working on a large codebase, or a hobbyist building personal projects, having a scalable organization strategy is essential for long-term success.

Key concepts and terminology introduced in this chapter include "modularity," "package boundaries," "dependency management," "code coupling," and "separation of concerns." We'll explain these terms using real-world analogies—for example, comparing a monolithic codebase to a large, cluttered warehouse versus a modular codebase being like a series of well-labeled, neatly organized storage units. This analogy helps illustrate why breaking your code into manageable pieces makes it easier to find what you need, change components independently, and scale up your project over time.

Throughout this chapter, we will discuss:

- **Best practices for project organization:** How to split your code into packages and modules that reflect logical boundaries.

- **Tips for maintainability:** Strategies for keeping your codebase clean as new features are added.

- **Refactoring techniques:** How to convert a monolithic project into a modular design without disrupting functionality.

- **Real-world examples:** Detailed walkthroughs of code examples that show you how to restructure a project, manage dependencies, and enforce clear interfaces between modules.

The chapter is designed to be both theoretical and practical. After establishing a solid conceptual foundation, we'll dive into hands-on examples. One such example will be a refactoring exercise that transforms a monolithic project into a modular design. You will see code before and after refactoring, and learn why each change improves maintainability and scalability.

By the end of this chapter, you will understand the importance of organizing code for scalability and be equipped with practical strategies to structure your Go projects effectively. With clear guidance and actionable insights, you'll be able to design systems that not only perform well under load but also evolve gracefully as requirements change over time.

Let's now explore the core concepts that underpin scalable code organization in Go.

2. Core Concepts and Theory

Effective code organization is founded on several core principles that promote modularity, loose coupling, and clarity. In this section, we'll break down these principles and illustrate how they apply to Go programming.

2.1. Modularity and Separation of Concerns

Modularity refers to breaking a program into distinct, self-contained components (modules) that encapsulate specific functionality. Each module is responsible for a well-defined aspect of the application, and modules interact with each other through clear interfaces.

- **Separation of Concerns:**
  This principle encourages you to split your code based on different responsibilities. For example, you might separate database access logic from business logic, and both from the

presentation layer. In Go, this is often achieved by organizing code into packages.

Real-World Analogy:

Think of a well-organized kitchen. Instead of having one counter where every task is performed, you have separate areas for preparing ingredients, cooking, and plating. Each station has a clear purpose, making the workflow efficient and less error-prone.

2.2. Package Boundaries and Dependency Management

In Go, packages are the unit of modularity. A package groups related functionality together and defines a clear boundary through its exported and unexported identifiers. This allows you to control which functions and types are accessible to other parts of your program.

- **Exported vs. Unexported:**
  By convention, identifiers that start with an uppercase letter are exported (public), while those starting with a lowercase letter are unexported (private). This mechanism enforces encapsulation, ensuring that internal details remain hidden.

- **Managing Dependencies:**
  As your project grows, managing dependencies between packages becomes critical. Use Go modules to specify versioned dependencies, ensuring that your project builds consistently regardless of external changes.

Real-World Analogy:

Imagine each package as a department in a large organization. Each department has its own set of internal processes (unexported identifiers) but provides services to other departments through a defined interface (exported identifiers).

2.3. Designing for Maintainability

Maintainable code is easier to understand, modify, and extend. Here are key practices for maintainability:

- Keep functions and methods small and focused.

- Write clear, descriptive names for functions, variables, and packages.

- Document public interfaces and expected behavior using comments.

- Avoid deep nesting by breaking complex logic into helper functions.

- Adopt a consistent coding style and use tools like gofmt for formatting.

Example:

Instead of writing a single massive function that handles multiple steps of a process, break it into smaller helper functions—each responsible for one aspect. This not only makes the code more readable but also simplifies testing.

2.4. Refactoring Monolithic Projects

Refactoring is the process of restructuring existing code without changing its external behavior. A monolithic project, where all code resides in a single module or package, can become difficult to manage as it grows. Refactoring into a modular design involves:

- **Identifying logical boundaries:**
  Determine which parts of the code can be separated into independent packages.

- **Defining clear interfaces:**
  Ensure that communication between packages occurs via well-defined interfaces.

- **Gradually extracting code:**
  Refactor incrementally to avoid breaking functionality.

- **Testing throughout:**
  Use tests to confirm that behavior remains consistent during refactoring.

Real-World Example:

Imagine a legacy application that handles everything—from user authentication to data processing—in one giant file. By refactoring, you might split the code into separate packages like auth, db, handlers, and utils, each with its own set of responsibilities.

2.5. Dependency Injection and Inversion of Control

Dependency injection is a design pattern where dependencies are provided to a component rather than hardcoded within it. This pattern is useful for making code more testable and decoupled. In Go, dependency injection can be implemented manually by passing dependencies (such as configurations or service interfaces) to functions or constructors.

- **Benefits:**

    o Reduces coupling between components.

    o Makes testing easier by allowing you to substitute mocks.

    o Improves code flexibility.

Real-World Analogy:
Consider a car manufacturing process. Instead of the assembly line building its own engines, engines are provided by specialized suppliers. This separation allows the car manufacturer to focus on assembly while using the best available engines from external vendors.

2.6. Strategies for Scalable Code Organization

To summarize the core concepts:

- **Emphasize modularity:**
    Organize your code into well-defined packages with clear responsibilities.

- **Control dependencies:**

  Use Go modules and careful design to manage dependencies between packages.

- **Encapsulate functionality:**

  Hide internal details behind exported interfaces.

- **Refactor incrementally:**

  Gradually split monolithic code into smaller, more manageable units.

- **Adopt dependency injection:**

  Pass dependencies into functions and constructors to reduce coupling.

These concepts are not unique to Go; they're fundamental principles in software engineering. However, Go's package system, built-in tools, and conventions make it easier to implement these practices effectively.

---

3. Tools and Setup

Before diving into practical examples, it's essential to set up your development environment with the right tools. In this section, we detail the software, editors, and version control systems that will help you organize your code for scalability.

3.1. Software Requirements

For this chapter, ensure you have:

- **Go Compiler and Runtime:** Download the latest version from the official Go website.

- **Integrated Development Environment (IDE) or Text Editor:** Recommended editors include Visual Studio Code, GoLand, or Sublime Text with Go language support.

- **Command-Line Interface:** Use Terminal on macOS/Linux or Command Prompt/PowerShell on Windows.

- **Version Control System:** Git is highly recommended for tracking changes and collaborating with others.

- **Dependency Management:** Go modules (go.mod and go.sum) are built-in to manage external libraries.

3.2. Configuring Your IDE

A well-configured IDE can drastically improve your productivity. For example, if you're using Visual Studio Code:

1. **Install VS Code:** Download from code.visualstudio.com and install it.

2. **Add the Go Extension:** Open the Extensions pane (Ctrl+Shift+X), search for "Go," and install the official extension.

3. **Set Up Formatting:** Ensure that gofmt or goimports is configured to format your code automatically on save.

4. **Enable Code Navigation:** Use features like "Go to Definition" and "Find References" to navigate through your packages.

5. **Workspace Organization:** Create a workspace folder (e.g., go-scalability) where your projects will reside.

3.3. Command-Line Tools

Make sure your command-line environment is set up for Go development:

- **Verify Installation:** Run:

bash

```
go version
```
This should display the installed Go version.

- **Build and Test:** Familiarize yourself with basic commands:

bash

```
go build
go run main.go
go test -v ./...
```
- **Module Initialization:** Initialize a new Go module for your project:

bash

```
go mod init github.com/yourusername/go-scalability
```

3.4. Version Control Setup

Using Git to manage your code is a best practice, especially as projects grow:

- **Initialize Repository:** In your project folder:

```bash
git init
git add .
git commit -m "Initial commit: Project structure for scalability"
```

- **Branching Strategy:** Consider using feature branches for refactoring or new modules. This helps keep your main branch stable while you experiment with changes.

3.5. Project Organization

A clear directory structure is key to maintainability and scalability. One recommended structure is:

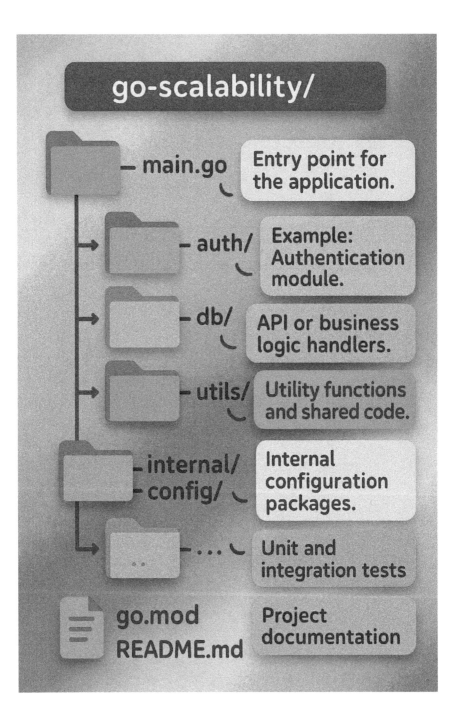

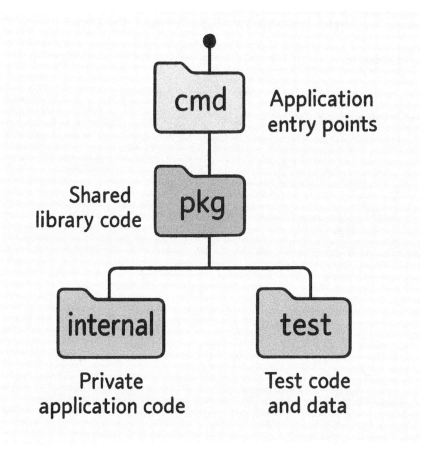

4. Hands-on Examples & Projects

This section provides a detailed walkthrough of practical examples and a complete project to illustrate how to organize code for scalability. We'll start with simple examples and gradually build a real-world example that refactors a monolithic project into a modular design.

4.1. Simple Example: Organizing a Utility Package

Imagine you have a utility function for string manipulation. Instead of embedding it in your main package, you can create a separate package for utilities.

Step 1: Create a Utility Package

In the /pkg/utils folder, create stringutils.go:

```go
package utils

// Reverse returns the reversed string of s.
func Reverse(s string) string {
    r := []rune(s)
    for i, j := 0, len(r)-1; i < j; i, j = i+1, j-1 {
        r[i], r[j] = r[j], r[i]
    }
    return string(r)
}
```
Explanation:

This utility package defines a simple function for reversing strings. By isolating it in its own package, you make it reusable across your application.

Step 2: Use the Utility Package in Your Main Program

In /cmd/main.go:

```go
package main

import (
```

```go
    "fmt"
    "github.com/yourusername/go-
scalability/pkg/utils"
)

func main() {
    input := "scalable"
    output := utils.Reverse(input)
    fmt.Printf("Original: %s, Reversed: %s\n", input,
output)
}
```

4.2. Refactoring a Monolithic Project: The Before Scenario

Consider a monolithic project where all code is contained in a single large file. This file handles everything from HTTP routing to business logic, data access, and error handling. Such a design might work initially, but as the project grows, it becomes hard to maintain.

Before Example:

```go
go

// monolithic.go
package main

import (
    "fmt"
    "net/http"
)

func main() {
    http.HandleFunc("/hello", func(w
http.ResponseWriter, r *http.Request) {
        fmt.Fprintln(w, "Hello, World!")
    })
    // Additional handlers and business logic
embedded here...
    http.ListenAndServe(":8080", nil)
```

}
Problems with this Approach:

- **Lack of Modularity:** All functionality is in one file, making it hard to locate specific features.

- **Difficult Testing:** Tightly coupled code is hard to test in isolation.

- **Poor Maintainability:** As new features are added, the file grows unmanageably large.

4.3. Refactoring into a Modular Design: The After Scenario

The goal is to refactor the monolithic project into a modular design with clear package boundaries. We will split the code into multiple packages— each with a well-defined responsibility.

Step 1: Create Separate Packages

For example:

- **/cmd/main.go:** The entry point for the application.

- **/pkg/handlers/handlers.go:** Contains HTTP handlers.

- **/pkg/server/server.go:** Contains server initialization and configuration.

- **/pkg/utils/utils.go:** Contains shared utility functions.

After Refactoring:

File: /pkg/handlers/handlers.go

```go

package handlers

import (
    "encoding/json"
    "net/http"
)

// HelloHandler responds with a welcome message.
func HelloHandler(w http.ResponseWriter, r *http.Request) {
    response := map[string]string{"message": "Hello, World!"}
    w.Header().Set("Content-Type", "application/json")
    json.NewEncoder(w).Encode(response)
}
```

File: /pkg/server/server.go

```go

package server

import (
    "log"
    "net/http"

    "github.com/yourusername/go-scalability/pkg/handlers"
)

// StartServer initializes HTTP routes and starts the server.
func StartServer(port string) {
    http.HandleFunc("/hello", handlers.HelloHandler)
    log.Printf("Server running on port %s\n", port)
    log.Fatal(http.ListenAndServe(":"+port, nil))
}
```

File: /cmd/main.go

```go

```

```
package main

import "github.com/yourusername/go-
scalability/pkg/server"

func main() {
    server.StartServer("8080")
}
```

Explanation:

This modular design separates concerns neatly. HTTP handlers, server configuration, and the main entry point are in distinct packages. This structure enhances maintainability, facilitates testing, and allows teams to work on different parts independently.

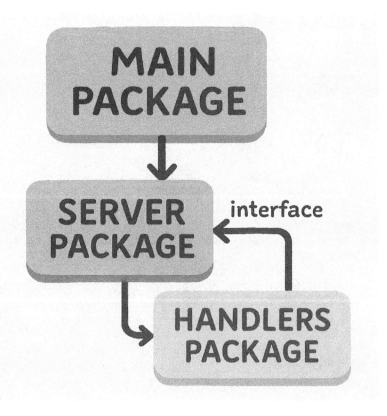

4.4. Real-World Project: Developing a Scalable API

We will now develop a small API using this modular design approach. The API will include endpoints for basic CRUD operations. We'll focus on organizing the code to make it scalable and maintainable as features grow.

Project Overview

Objective:
Build a small API that supports:

- Retrieving a list of items.

- Adding new items.

- Updating existing items.

- Deleting items.

Design Goals:

- **Modular Architecture:** Split the API into separate packages for routing, business logic, data access, and utilities.

- **Maintainability:** Ensure that each package has a single responsibility.

- **Testability:** Write tests for each component so that changes in one module do not affect others.

Step 1: Define the Data Model and Business Logic

File: /pkg/api/model.go

```go
package api

// Item represents a resource in the API.
type Item struct {
    ID      int     `json:"id"`
    Name    string  `json:"name"`
    Value   string  `json:"value"`
}
```

File: /pkg/api/service.go

```go
package api

import (
    "errors"
    "sync"
)

// Service provides business logic for managing
items.
type Service struct {
    mu      sync.RWMutex
    items   map[int]Item
    nextID  int
}

// NewService creates a new Service instance.
func NewService() *Service {
    return &Service{
        items: make(map[int]Item),
        nextID: 1,
    }
}

// GetAll retrieves all items.
func (s *Service) GetAll() []Item {
```

```go
    s.mu.RLock()
    defer s.mu.RUnlock()
    result := make([]Item, 0, len(s.items))
    for _, item := range s.items {
        result = append(result, item)
    }
    return result
}

// AddItem adds a new item.
func (s *Service) AddItem(name, value string) Item {
    s.mu.Lock()
    defer s.mu.Unlock()
    item := Item{ID: s.nextID, Name: name, Value:
value}
    s.items[s.nextID] = item
    s.nextID++
    return item
}

// UpdateItem updates an existing item.
func (s *Service) UpdateItem(id int, name, value
string) (Item, error) {
    s.mu.Lock()
    defer s.mu.Unlock()
    item, exists := s.items[id]
    if !exists {
        return Item{}, errors.New("item not found")
    }
    item.Name = name
    item.Value = value
    s.items[id] = item
    return item, nil
}

// DeleteItem removes an item.
func (s *Service) DeleteItem(id int) error {
    s.mu.Lock()
    defer s.mu.Unlock()
    if _, exists := s.items[id]; !exists {
        return errors.New("item not found")
    }
    delete(s.items, id)
    return nil
```

```
}
```

Explanation:

The API package defines a simple in-memory data model and business logic with concurrency safety via mutexes. This design ensures that the core functionality is isolated and easily testable.

Step 2: Create HTTP Handlers for the API

File: /pkg/handlers/api_handlers.go

```go
package handlers

import (
    "encoding/json"
    "net/http"
    "strconv"

    "github.com/yourusername/go-scalability/pkg/api"
)

// APIHandler wraps the Service to provide HTTP
endpoints.
type APIHandler struct {
    Service *api.Service
}

// NewAPIHandler creates a new APIHandler instance.
func NewAPIHandler(service *api.Service) *APIHandler
{
    return &APIHandler{Service: service}
}

// GetItems handles GET requests to retrieve all
items.
func (h *APIHandler) GetItems(w http.ResponseWriter,
r *http.Request) {
    items := h.Service.GetAll()
    w.Header().Set("Content-Type",
"application/json")
```

```go
    json.NewEncoder(w).Encode(items)
}

// AddItem handles POST requests to add a new item.
func (h *APIHandler) AddItem(w http.ResponseWriter, r
*http.Request) {
    var input struct {
        Name   string `json:"name"`
        Value string `json:"value"`
    }
    if err := json.NewDecoder(r.Body).Decode(&input);
err != nil {
        http.Error(w, "Invalid input",
http.StatusBadRequest)
        return
    }
    item := h.Service.AddItem(input.Name,
input.Value)
    w.Header().Set("Content-Type",
"application/json")
    w.WriteHeader(http.StatusCreated)
    json.NewEncoder(w).Encode(item)
}

// UpdateItem handles PUT requests to update an item.
func (h *APIHandler) UpdateItem(w
http.ResponseWriter, r *http.Request) {
    idStr := r.URL.Query().Get("id")
    id, err := strconv.Atoi(idStr)
    if err != nil {
        http.Error(w, "Invalid ID",
http.StatusBadRequest)
        return
    }
    var input struct {
        Name   string `json:"name"`
        Value string `json:"value"`
    }
    if err := json.NewDecoder(r.Body).Decode(&input);
err != nil {
        http.Error(w, "Invalid input",
http.StatusBadRequest)
        return
    }
```

```
    updatedItem, err := h.Service.UpdateItem(id,
input.Name, input.Value)
    if err != nil {
        http.Error(w, err.Error(),
http.StatusNotFound)
        return
    }
    w.Header().Set("Content-Type",
"application/json")
    json.NewEncoder(w).Encode(updatedItem)
}

// DeleteItem handles DELETE requests to remove an
item.
func (h *APIHandler) DeleteItem(w
http.ResponseWriter, r *http.Request) {
    idStr := r.URL.Query().Get("id")
    id, err := strconv.Atoi(idStr)
    if err != nil {
        http.Error(w, "Invalid ID",
http.StatusBadRequest)
        return
    }
    if err := h.Service.DeleteItem(id); err != nil {
        http.Error(w, err.Error(),
http.StatusNotFound)
        return
    }
    w.WriteHeader(http.StatusNoContent)
}
```

Explanation:

The handlers package exposes **HTTP** endpoints that wrap the business logic in the **API** service. Each handler validates input, calls the appropriate service method, and handles errors gracefully, returning meaningful HTTP responses.

Step 3: Wiring Everything Together in the Main Server

File: /cmd/main.go

```go
package main

import (
    "log"
    "net/http"

    "github.com/yourusername/go-scalability/pkg/api"
    "github.com/yourusername/go-scalability/pkg/handlers"
)

func main() {
    service := api.NewService()
    apiHandler := handlers.NewAPIHandler(service)

    // Set up HTTP routes.
    http.HandleFunc("/items", func(w
http.ResponseWriter, r *http.Request) {
        switch r.Method {
        case http.MethodGet:
            apiHandler.GetItems(w, r)
        case http.MethodPost:
            apiHandler.AddItem(w, r)
        case http.MethodPut:
            apiHandler.UpdateItem(w, r)
        case http.MethodDelete:
            apiHandler.DeleteItem(w, r)
        default:
            http.Error(w, "Method not allowed",
http.StatusMethodNotAllowed)
        }
    })

    log.Println("API server is running on port
8080...")
    log.Fatal(http.ListenAndServe(":8080", nil))
}
```

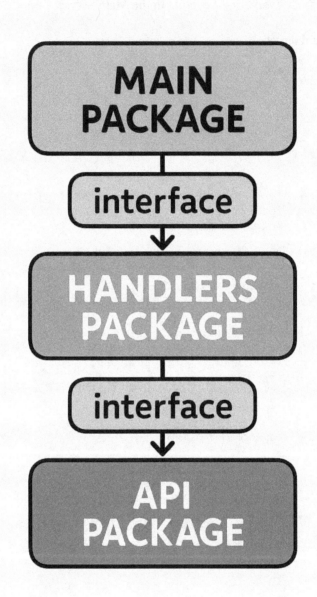

4.5. Testing the Modular API

Thorough testing is critical. Create test files (e.g., /test/api_test.go) to validate each endpoint's behavior. We already saw examples in earlier chapters; here's a summary:

- **Test for Adding an Item:** Send a POST request and verify that the response contains the expected item.

- **Test for Retrieving Items:** Add an item, then send a GET request and verify that the list contains that item.

- **Test for Updating and Deleting Items:** Simulate update and delete operations and check the responses for correctness.

Example Test:

```go
package api_test

import (
    "bytes"
    "encoding/json"
    "net/http"
    "net/http/httptest"
    "strconv"
    "testing"

    "github.com/yourusername/go-scalability/pkg/api"
    "github.com/yourusername/go-
scalability/pkg/handlers"
)

func TestAddItem(t *testing.T) {
    service := api.NewService()
    handler := handlers.NewAPIHandler(service)
```

```
    payload := []byte(`{"name": "TestItem", "value":
"TestValue"}`)
    req, err := http.NewRequest("POST", "/items",
bytes.NewBuffer(payload))
    if err != nil {
        t.Fatal(err)
    }
    rr := httptest.NewRecorder()
    handler.AddItem(rr, req)

    if status := rr.Code; status !=
http.StatusCreated {
        t.Errorf("Expected status code %d, got %d",
http.StatusCreated, status)
    }

    var item api.Item
    if err := json.Unmarshal(rr.Body.Bytes(), &item);
err != nil {
        t.Fatal(err)
    }

    if item.Name != "TestItem" {
        t.Errorf("Expected item name 'TestItem', got
'%s'", item.Name)
    }
}
```
Explanation:

This test ensures that the AddItem endpoint correctly creates and returns a new item. Similar tests can be written for other endpoints.

---

5 . Conclusion & Next Steps

This chapter has provided an extensive guide to organizing your Go code for scalability. We began by discussing the importance of modularity and separation of concerns—key principles that ensure your codebase remains maintainable as it grows. By defining clear package boundaries, managing dependencies effectively, and employing refactoring techniques, you can transform a monolithic project into a well-organized, modular system.

We explored core concepts such as dependency injection, interface-based design, and best practices for maintainability. Detailed examples illustrated how to create utility packages, refactor a monolithic API into distinct modules, and build a scalable API with separate layers for data access, business logic, and HTTP routing. We also discussed advanced optimization techniques and provided troubleshooting strategies to help you address common pitfalls.

As you move forward, consider these next steps:

- **Continue Refactoring:**
  Review your existing projects and look for opportunities to apply modular design principles.

- **Integrate CI/CD:**
  Automate testing and deployment processes to catch issues early and streamline your development workflow.

- **Study Advanced Patterns:**
  Explore design patterns like microservices architecture, dependency injection frameworks, and plugin systems to further enhance scalability.

- **Contribute to Open Source:**
  Engage with the Go community and contribute to projects that emphasize scalable code organization. This experience will expose you to a variety of design approaches and best practices.

- **Keep Learning:**

  Follow blogs, read books, and participate in online forums to stay updated on emerging trends and techniques in scalable software design.

Reflect on the transformation from a monolithic codebase to a modular design. The ability to decompose a large, unwieldy system into manageable components is a critical skill that will serve you well as projects evolve. Well-organized code not only makes development more efficient but also lays a strong foundation for future innovation and growth.

Thank you for working through this chapter on organizing code for scalability. The principles and practices you've learned here—combined with hands-on examples and real-world refactoring techniques—will help you design systems that are robust, maintainable, and ready to scale as your projects and teams grow.

May your packages be well-structured, your dependencies managed cleanly, and your code remain elegant and scalable. Happy coding, and best of luck as you apply these principles to build the next generation of high-performance Go applications!

Chapter 11: Building Web Services and APIs

1. Introduction

In today's digital landscape, web services and APIs are the backbone of modern applications. They allow disparate systems to communicate and share data over the internet, enabling developers to build powerful, scalable, and modular systems. In Go, creating RESTful services is not only straightforward but also highly efficient, thanks to the language's built-in support for HTTP, JSON handling, and a robust standard library.

This chapter delves into building web services and APIs using Go. We'll start by exploring why web services matter and what distinguishes RESTful APIs from other communication protocols. You'll learn key concepts and terminology—such as endpoints, HTTP methods, routing, and JSON—and understand how they contribute to building reliable and maintainable systems. By the end of this chapter, you'll appreciate why well-structured APIs can simplify application development and foster integration between services.

We will discuss the significance of separating concerns, where routing, business logic, and data access are divided into well-defined modules. This approach not only improves code clarity and maintainability but also facilitates collaboration in team environments. Whether you're planning to build a public API for third-party developers or a private API to support your own web application, mastering these concepts is critical.

In our discussion, you'll see how Go's simplicity is leveraged to build robust web services. The language's minimal syntax, efficient concurrency model, and comprehensive standard library make it an ideal choice for developing scalable APIs. We'll look at examples that illustrate how to use the net/http package for routing, how to encode and decode JSON payloads, and how to handle errors gracefully—ensuring that your API provides meaningful responses even in the face of unexpected conditions.

The chapter is designed to be both theoretical and highly practical. After discussing the core concepts, we'll cover the tools and setup required to build web services, including your preferred IDE, command-line tools, and version control systems. Next, you'll follow a step-by-step walkthrough of a hands-on project—a simple web service that supports basic CRUD operations. This exercise demonstrates real-world techniques, such as routing requests to handlers, managing request data, and integrating with external systems like databases or other APIs.

Throughout the chapter, we maintain a professional, yet approachable tone. Every technical term is defined clearly, and complex ideas are broken down into digestible pieces using real-world analogies. For instance, think of your API as a restaurant: endpoints are like menu items, HTTP methods are the actions you take (ordering, updating, or canceling a meal), and JSON is the language that servers use to describe your order. Just as a well-run restaurant requires an organized kitchen and clear communication between staff, a well-designed API needs clear structure and robust error handling.

By the end of this chapter, you'll have a deep understanding of how to build web services and APIs in Go. You'll be comfortable with setting up routes, handling JSON data, integrating with external databases, and writing tests to ensure your API works as expected. Whether you are new to web development or looking to expand your backend skills, the knowledge you gain here will empower you to build scalable, efficient, and maintainable web services.

Let's begin by exploring the core concepts behind RESTful services and the fundamental building blocks that make up an API in Go.

2. Core Concepts and Theory

This section provides detailed explanations of the foundational concepts behind web services and APIs in Go. We'll cover REST principles, HTTP methods, routing, JSON encoding/decoding, and integration with databases and external APIs.

2.1. RESTful Web Services

REST, or Representational State Transfer, is an architectural style that emphasizes stateless communication and the use of standard HTTP methods. RESTful services expose resources (such as user data or products) via unique URLs and allow clients to interact with these resources using standard operations.

- **Endpoints and Resources:**
  Each resource in your API is represented by a unique URL (endpoint). For example, /users might represent a collection of users, while /users/123 represents a specific user.

- **HTTP Methods:**
  RESTful APIs typically use the following methods:

  o **GET:** Retrieve data from the server.

  o **POST:** Create a new resource.

  o **PUT:** Update an existing resource.

  o **DELETE:** Remove a resource.
     These methods align closely with CRUD operations (Create, Read, Update, Delete).

- **Statelessness:**
  In REST, every request from a client must contain all the information needed to understand and process the request. The server does not store client context between requests, which simplifies scaling and improves reliability.

Real-World Analogy:
Imagine a library. Each book (resource) has a unique call number (endpoint). Patrons (clients) request books (GET), add new books (POST), update book information (PUT), or remove books (DELETE). The librarian (server) processes each request independently, without needing to remember previous interactions with a patron.

2.2. HTTP and Routing

HTTP is the protocol used by web services to transfer data over the internet. In Go, the net/http package is the workhorse for creating web servers and handling HTTP requests.

- **Routing:**
  Routing refers to directing incoming HTTP requests to the appropriate handler functions. Handlers are functions that process the request, perform necessary operations, and write a response.

- **Handler Functions:**
  A handler function in Go has the signature func(w http.ResponseWriter, r *http.Request). The ResponseWriter is used to send data back to the client, while the Request contains all the information about the incoming request.

- **Middleware:**
  Middleware functions act as intermediaries that process requests before they reach your handlers. They can be used for tasks like logging, authentication, or modifying request data.

2.3. JSON Encoding and Decoding

JSON (JavaScript Object Notation) is the most common data format for exchanging information in web services. Go's encoding/json package provides functions to easily encode Go data structures into JSON and decode JSON into Go data structures.

- **Encoding:**

  Converting a Go struct or map into a JSON string using json.NewEncoder(w).Encode(data).

- **Decoding:**

  Parsing JSON from a request body into a Go struct using json.NewDecoder(r.Body).Decode(&struct).

Real-World Analogy:

Think of JSON as a universal language that allows different systems to understand each other. Just like translating a document from one language to another, encoding converts your Go data into JSON for transmission, and decoding translates JSON back into Go data.

2.4. Integrating with Databases and External APIs

Modern web services often need to store data persistently or interact with external systems. In Go, you can integrate with databases using libraries such as database/sql and drivers like pq for PostgreSQL or mysql for MySQL. Similarly, calling external APIs can be done using the net/http package.

- **Database Integration:**

  Establish a connection to your database, execute queries, and manage transactions. Ensure that error handling is robust to deal with connectivity issues or query failures.

- **External API Integration:**
  Make HTTP requests to third-party services, handle JSON responses, and integrate data into your application. This might involve setting timeouts, managing authentication, and parsing responses.

2.5. Error Handling in Web Services

In a web service, error handling is paramount. Not only must you capture errors, but you should also return meaningful HTTP status codes and messages. For instance:

- **400 Bad Request:** For malformed input.

- **404 Not Found:** For non-existent resources.

- **500 Internal Server Error:** For unexpected issues on the server side.

By handling errors gracefully, you improve the user experience and make it easier to diagnose issues.

Real-World Example:
A payment processing API should clearly indicate whether a transaction failed due to invalid input, insufficient funds, or a system error. Detailed error responses help clients understand and remedy issues quickly.

2.6. Testing Web Services

Testing is essential to ensure that your API behaves correctly under different scenarios. In Go, the testing package, along with tools like httptest, enables you to write unit tests and integration tests for your endpoints.

- **Unit Tests:**

    Test individual functions and handlers in isolation.

- **Integration Tests:**

    Simulate actual HTTP requests and check the responses.

- **Table-Driven Tests:**

    Run multiple test cases through the same test function to cover a wide range of inputs and scenarios.

These tests ensure that your API remains reliable as you refactor and add new features.

---

3. Tools and Setup

Before building your web service, it's important to set up your development environment correctly. This section provides a step-by-step guide to configuring your tools and organizing your project.

3.1. Software Requirements

For building web services and APIs with Go, you'll need:

- **Go Compiler and Runtime:** Download the latest version from the official Go website.

- **Integrated Development Environment (IDE) or Code Editor:**
  Visual Studio Code, GoLand, or Sublime Text with Go support.

- **Command-Line Interface:** Terminal (macOS/Linux) or
  Command Prompt/PowerShell (Windows).

- **Version Control System:** Git for managing your code and
  collaborating with others.

- **Database Driver (Optional):** If integrating with a database, install
  the appropriate driver (e.g., pq for PostgreSQL, mysql for
  MySQL).

3.2. Configuring Your IDE

For a smooth development experience, configure your IDE to work well
with Go and web development:

1. **Install Your IDE:** For instance, download Visual Studio Code
   from code.visualstudio.com.

2. **Add the Go Extension:**
   Open the Extensions pane (Ctrl+Shift+X), search for "Go," and
   install the official Go extension.

3. **Set Up Formatting and Linting:**
   Enable gofmt and golint in your settings to maintain consistent
   code style.

4. **Configure Debugging:**

   Set up your debugger (e.g., Delve) to step through your code, which is especially useful when troubleshooting web services.

5. **Create a Workspace:**

   Organize your project in a dedicated folder, such as go-webservices, and structure your files according to best practices (as described later).

3.3. Command-Line Tools and Environment Setup

Ensure that your terminal is ready for Go development:

- **Verify Installation:**

   Run:

```bash

go version
```
This command should output the installed Go version.

- **Build and Run Commands:**

   Familiarize yourself with:

```bash

go run main.go
go build
go test -v ./...
```
- **Module Initialization:**

   Initialize a new Go module in your project directory:

```bash
```

```
go mod init github.com/yourusername/go-webservices
```
This creates a go.mod file that helps manage dependencies.

3.4. Version Control and Project Organization

Using Git is essential for tracking changes and collaborating on your code:

- **Initialize Git:**

  In your project folder:

```bash

git init
git add .
git commit -m "Initial commit: Setup for building web
services"
```
- **Directory Structure:**

  Organize your project into meaningful directories. A

  recommended structure is:

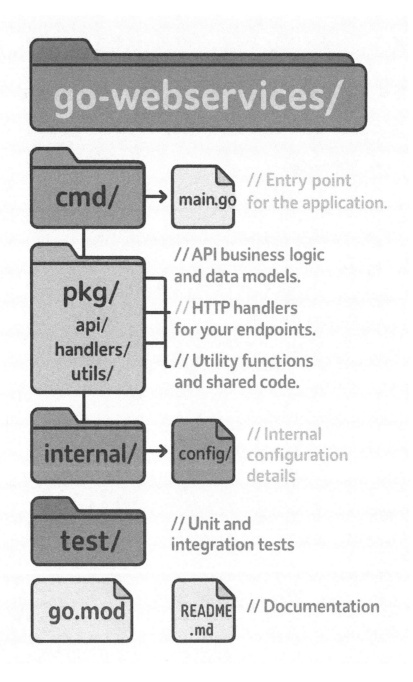

4. Hands-on Examples & Projects

In this section, we will walk through practical examples and build a complete web service project that demonstrates the concepts discussed. We'll cover routing, JSON handling, and integration with external systems.

4.1. Simple Web Service: An Overview

Our first example is a simple web service that exposes a single endpoint. This endpoint will handle a GET request and return a JSON response. We will start with a basic setup and gradually add more functionality.

Example: Hello World API

```go
package main

import (
    "encoding/json"
    "log"
    "net/http"
)

// Response defines the structure for JSON responses.
type Response struct {
    Message string `json:"message"`
}

func helloHandler(w http.ResponseWriter, r
*http.Request) {
    w.Header().Set("Content-Type",
"application/json")
    response := Response{Message: "Hello, World!"}
    json.NewEncoder(w).Encode(response)
}
```

```go
func main() {
    http.HandleFunc("/hello", helloHandler)
    log.Println("Server is running on port 8080...")
    log.Fatal(http.ListenAndServe(":8080", nil))
}
```

Explanation:

This simple API listens on port 8080 and responds to GET requests at /hello with a JSON message. Notice how JSON encoding is done using json.NewEncoder.

4.2. Integrating with External APIs

Before building a full API, let's see how to make an HTTP request to an external API. This is useful when your service needs to consume data from third-party services.

Example: Consuming an External API

```go
go

package main

import (
    "encoding/json"
    "fmt"
    "log"
    "net/http"
)

type Joke struct {
    Setup     string `json:"setup"`
    Punchline string `json:"punchline"`
}

func getJoke() (*Joke, error) {
    resp, err := http.Get("https://official-joke-api.appspot.com/random_joke")
    if err != nil {
```

```
        return nil, err
    }
    defer resp.Body.Close()

    var joke Joke
    if err :=
json.NewDecoder(resp.Body).Decode(&joke); err != nil
{
        return nil, err
    }
    return &joke, nil
}

func main() {
    joke, err := getJoke()
    if err != nil {
        log.Fatalf("Error fetching joke: %v", err)
    }
    fmt.Printf("Joke: %s - %s\n", joke.Setup,
joke.Punchline)
}
```

Explanation:

This example makes an HTTP GET request to an external joke API, decodes the JSON response into a Joke struct, and prints the result.

4.3. Building a Complete RESTful API

We now combine the concepts from the previous sections to build a small RESTful API. Our API will support basic CRUD operations on a collection of items. We'll structure the project into modules, handle JSON requests/responses, and implement proper error handling.

Step 1: Defining the Data Model and Service Layer

In the /pkg/api directory, create the following files.

File: model.go

```go
go

package api

// Item represents a resource in the API.
type Item struct {
    ID      int     `json:"id"`
    Name    string  `json:"name"`
    Value   string  `json:"value"`
}
```

File: service.go

```go
go

package api

import (
    "errors"
    "sync"
)

// Service provides business logic for managing
items.
type Service struct {
    mu      sync.RWMutex
    items   map[int]Item
    nextID  int
}

// NewService creates a new Service instance.
func NewService() *Service {
    return &Service{
        items:  make(map[int]Item),
        nextID: 1,
    }
}

// GetAll retrieves all items.
func (s *Service) GetAll() []Item {
    s.mu.RLock()
    defer s.mu.RUnlock()
    result := make([]Item, 0, len(s.items))
    for _, item := range s.items {
```

```go
        result = append(result, item)
    }
    return result
}

// AddItem adds a new item.
func (s *Service) AddItem(name, value string) Item {
    s.mu.Lock()
    defer s.mu.Unlock()
    item := Item{ID: s.nextID, Name: name, Value:
value}
    s.items[s.nextID] = item
    s.nextID++
    return item
}

// UpdateItem updates an existing item.
func (s *Service) UpdateItem(id int, name, value
string) (Item, error) {
    s.mu.Lock()
    defer s.mu.Unlock()
    item, exists := s.items[id]
    if !exists {
        return Item{}, errors.New("item not found")
    }
    item.Name = name
    item.Value = value
    s.items[id] = item
    return item, nil
}

// DeleteItem removes an item.
func (s *Service) DeleteItem(id int) error {
    s.mu.Lock()
    defer s.mu.Unlock()
    if _, exists := s.items[id]; !exists {
        return errors.New("item not found")
    }
    delete(s.items, id)
    return nil
}
```

Step 2: Creating HTTP Handlers

In the /pkg/handlers directory, create handlers.go:

```go
package handlers

import (
    "encoding/json"
    "net/http"
    "strconv"

    "github.com/yourusername/go-webservices/pkg/api"
)

// APIHandler wraps the Service for handling HTTP
requests.
type APIHandler struct {
    Service *api.Service
}

// NewAPIHandler creates a new APIHandler.
func NewAPIHandler(service *api.Service) *APIHandler
{
    return &APIHandler{Service: service}
}

// GetItems handles GET requests to retrieve all
items.
func (h *APIHandler) GetItems(w http.ResponseWriter,
r *http.Request) {
    items := h.Service.GetAll()
    w.Header().Set("Content-Type",
"application/json")
    json.NewEncoder(w).Encode(items)
}

// AddItem handles POST requests to add a new item.
func (h *APIHandler) AddItem(w http.ResponseWriter, r
*http.Request) {
    var input struct {
        Name   string `json:"name"`
```

```go
        Value string `json:"value"`
    }
    if err := json.NewDecoder(r.Body).Decode(&input);
err != nil {
        http.Error(w, "Invalid input",
http.StatusBadRequest)
        return
    }
    item := h.Service.AddItem(input.Name,
input.Value)
    w.Header().Set("Content-Type",
"application/json")
    w.WriteHeader(http.StatusCreated)
    json.NewEncoder(w).Encode(item)
}

// UpdateItem handles PUT requests to update an item.
func (h *APIHandler) UpdateItem(w
http.ResponseWriter, r *http.Request) {
    idStr := r.URL.Query().Get("id")
    id, err := strconv.Atoi(idStr)
    if err != nil {
        http.Error(w, "Invalid ID",
http.StatusBadRequest)
        return
    }
    var input struct {
        Name  string `json:"name"`
        Value string `json:"value"`
    }
    if err := json.NewDecoder(r.Body).Decode(&input);
err != nil {
        http.Error(w, "Invalid input",
http.StatusBadRequest)
        return
    }
    updatedItem, err := h.Service.UpdateItem(id,
input.Name, input.Value)
    if err != nil {
        http.Error(w, err.Error(),
http.StatusNotFound)
        return
    }
```

```go
    w.Header().Set("Content-Type",
"application/json")
    json.NewEncoder(w).Encode(updatedItem)
}

// DeleteItem handles DELETE requests to remove an
item.
func (h *APIHandler) DeleteItem(w
http.ResponseWriter, r *http.Request) {
    idStr := r.URL.Query().Get("id")
    id, err := strconv.Atoi(idStr)
    if err != nil {
        http.Error(w, "Invalid ID",
http.StatusBadRequest)
        return
    }
    if err := h.Service.DeleteItem(id); err != nil {
        http.Error(w, err.Error(),
http.StatusNotFound)
        return
    }
    w.WriteHeader(http.StatusNoContent)
}
```

Step 3: Main Server Setup

In the /cmd directory, create main.go:

```go
go

package main

import (
    "log"
    "net/http"

    "github.com/yourusername/go-webservices/pkg/api"
    "github.com/yourusername/go-
webservices/pkg/handlers"
)

func main() {
    service := api.NewService()
    apiHandler := handlers.NewAPIHandler(service)
```

```go
    http.HandleFunc("/items", func(w
http.ResponseWriter, r *http.Request) {
        switch r.Method {
        case http.MethodGet:
            apiHandler.GetItems(w, r)
        case http.MethodPost:
            apiHandler.AddItem(w, r)
        case http.MethodPut:
            apiHandler.UpdateItem(w, r)
        case http.MethodDelete:
            apiHandler.DeleteItem(w, r)
        default:
            http.Error(w, "Method not allowed",
http.StatusMethodNotAllowed)
        }
    })

    log.Println("API server is running on port
8080...")
    log.Fatal(http.ListenAndServe(":8080", nil))
}
```

4.4 Testing Your API

Testing is crucial. Create tests in the /test directory to ensure your endpoints work as expected. For instance, write tests for adding, updating, retrieving, and deleting items.

Example Test: Testing AddItem Endpoint

```go
package api_test

import (
    "bytes"
    "encoding/json"
    "net/http"
    "net/http/httptest"
    "testing"
```

```
    "github.com/yourusername/go-webservices/pkg/api"
    "github.com/yourusername/go-
webservices/pkg/handlers"
)

func TestAddItem(t *testing.T) {
    service := api.NewService()
    handler := handlers.NewAPIHandler(service)

    payload := []byte(`{"name": "TestItem", "value":
"TestValue"}`)
    req, err := http.NewRequest("POST", "/items",
bytes.NewBuffer(payload))
    if err != nil {
        t.Fatal(err)
    }
    rr := httptest.NewRecorder()
    handler.AddItem(rr, req)

    if status := rr.Code; status !=
http.StatusCreated {
        t.Errorf("handler returned wrong status code:
got %v want %v", status, http.StatusCreated)
    }

    var item api.Item
    if err := json.Unmarshal(rr.Body.Bytes(), &item);
err != nil {
        t.Fatal(err)
    }

    if item.Name != "TestItem" {
        t.Errorf("Expected item name 'TestItem', got
'%s'", item.Name)
    }
}
```

Explanation:

This test simulates a POST request to add an item and checks that the response matches expectations. Similar tests should be written for all endpoints.

5 . Conclusion & Next Steps

In this chapter, we've explored the process of building web services and APIs with Go. We began by discussing the importance of RESTful design, HTTP routing, and JSON handling. You learned how to create modular, scalable APIs that separate concerns across different packages—ensuring that your code remains maintainable as it grows.

We then examined how to integrate Go with external systems, such as databases and third-party APIs, and discussed best practices for error handling and returning meaningful responses. Through a hands-on project, you built a small API that supports basic CRUD operations. We detailed how to organize your code into packages for clear separation of concerns, how to write clean HTTP handlers, and how to test each endpoint thoroughly.

Advanced techniques such as middleware, dependency injection, caching, and performance profiling were also discussed, providing you with strategies to further optimize your web services. Finally, we covered troubleshooting and problem-solving tips to help you identify and resolve common issues that arise during development.

As you move forward, here are some recommended next steps:

- **Extend Your API:**
  Add new features and endpoints, integrate with a persistent database, and implement advanced middleware for logging, authentication, or rate limiting.

- **Adopt Test-Driven Development (TDD):**
  Write tests before implementing new features to ensure that your API remains robust and that changes do not introduce regressions.

- **Set Up CI/CD Pipelines:**
  Automate your testing and deployment processes using tools like GitHub Actions, Travis CI, or CircleCI.

- **Explore Advanced Frameworks:**
  Investigate third-party libraries such as Gorilla Mux for more flexible routing, or Echo for high-performance web frameworks.

- **Engage with the Community:**
  Participate in forums, contribute to open-source projects, and learn from other developers' experiences to refine your skills.

- **Keep Learning:**
  Read additional resources, attend workshops, and follow industry blogs to stay updated on best practices and emerging trends in web service development.

By applying these principles and techniques, you will be well-equipped to build scalable, maintainable, and high-performance web services. The journey from a simple "Hello, World!" API to a fully modular, production-ready system involves careful planning, continuous refactoring, and robust testing. The skills you've acquired in this chapter form the foundation for creating APIs that can grow with your needs and adapt to changing requirements.

Thank you for exploring this chapter on building web services and APIs with Go. As you continue your development journey, remember that a well-organized API not only makes your application easier to maintain but also paves the way for future expansion and integration with other systems. Embrace modular design, rigorous testing, and continuous improvement in your coding practices.

May your endpoints be responsive, your routes well-defined, and your JSON always valid. Happy coding, and best of luck as you build the next generation of scalable Go web services!

Chapter 12: Capstone Project – Building a Robust System

1. Introduction

In modern software development, it is not enough to write code that merely works; your code must be scalable, maintainable, and robust under varying conditions. As your applications grow in size and complexity, a well-architected design that integrates error handling, concurrency, modularity, and testing becomes indispensable. This chapter brings together all of these themes into one capstone project: building a complete system that addresses a common real-world challenge.

Imagine you're tasked with developing a system that manages a dynamic inventory for an online retailer. The system must handle multiple concurrent requests, interact with a database, expose a RESTful API for external integration, and gracefully handle errors while remaining easy to extend. In this chapter, we will design and build a similar robust system step-by-step, integrating topics from error handling and testing to concurrency and modular code organization.

Throughout the chapter, we define key concepts and terminology that you have encountered in earlier chapters—such as RESTful services, concurrency with goroutines, and modular design—and explain how they all fit together. You'll learn why designing a scalable system is so important and how using best practices now can save time and effort in the long run. We will explain the benefits of separating concerns, enforcing clear package boundaries, and testing each component thoroughly.

This capstone project is not just an academic exercise; it is a practical challenge that simulates real-world conditions. You will begin with a high-level design of the system, then gradually implement and integrate each component. We will start by outlining the project requirements and architecture, then move to the tools and setup needed for a productive development environment. From there, the chapter guides you through hands-on examples—from creating utility packages to refactoring monolithic code into modular components—culminating in a complete API that is well-tested and robust.

The tone throughout is professional and approachable. We break down complex ideas into clear, manageable sections, and we provide plenty of practical examples and annotated code snippets. Whether you are new to Go or a seasoned developer seeking to refine your architecture skills, this chapter is designed to challenge and guide you.

By the end of this chapter, you will have built a robust system that demonstrates how to:

- Organize code into modular, maintainable packages.

- Handle errors gracefully at every level of the application.

- Manage concurrent operations using goroutines and channels.

- Integrate with databases and external APIs.

- Write comprehensive tests for each component and endpoint.

- Refactor a monolithic codebase into a scalable, modular design.

With these skills, you will be equipped to tackle large-scale projects and ensure that your systems can grow and adapt over time. Let's begin by laying the conceptual foundation for designing robust, scalable systems in Go.

---

2. Core Concepts and Theory

To build a robust system, it is crucial to understand the foundational principles that guide scalable architecture. This section covers the theory behind modular design, error handling, concurrency, and testing—all key components of our final project.

2.1. Modular Design and Separation of Concerns

Modular design is the practice of breaking down a complex system into smaller, self-contained units (modules) that each handle a specific aspect of the overall functionality. This separation of concerns makes the code easier to understand, test, and maintain.

- **Modularity:**
  A modular system organizes related functionality into distinct packages. For example, you might have one package for API

handlers, another for business logic, and a third for data access. Each package has a clear responsibility.

- **Separation of Concerns:**
  This principle encourages developers to isolate different aspects of a system. When your business logic is decoupled from the web framework, changes to one part of the system are less likely to affect others. It also makes unit testing simpler since each module can be tested in isolation.

Real-World Analogy:
Think of a car assembly plant. Rather than having one massive department that builds everything, the process is divided into specialized areas such as engine assembly, bodywork, and painting. This specialization leads to higher quality and easier management.

2.2. Robust Error Handling

Error handling is a vital aspect of creating systems that are resilient to failure. In Go, errors are treated as explicit return values rather than exceptions, which forces you to consider error conditions at every step of your program.

- **Error as a Value:**
  Go functions return an error value along with their result. It is the caller's responsibility to check this error and decide how to handle it. This approach leads to more predictable and testable code.

- **Custom Errors:**
  Creating custom error types allows you to attach context to errors,

making it easier to diagnose and handle failures. For example, when interacting with a database, a custom error can include information about the failed query or connection details.

- **Error Propagation:**
  Functions should propagate errors up the call chain. This makes it possible to centralize error handling in higher-level functions, which might decide to log the error, retry the operation, or return an HTTP error code.

Real-World Analogy:
Consider a restaurant where each step of the process checks for problems. If the chef notices a spoiled ingredient, the problem is flagged immediately, and the dish is not sent out. This attention to error handling ensures that issues are caught early and addressed appropriately.

2.3. Concurrency and Scalability

Modern systems must handle multiple tasks concurrently to make full use of available hardware. Go provides lightweight goroutines and channels that simplify concurrent programming.

- **Goroutines:**
  Goroutines allow you to run functions concurrently. They are cheaper than traditional threads, making it possible to run thousands of them concurrently.

- **Channels:**
  Channels are used for communication between goroutines. They help to synchronize execution and exchange data safely,

preventing race conditions and ensuring that operations are executed in a coordinated manner.

- **Scalability Considerations:**
  A scalable system is one that can handle increasing loads without a proportional increase in complexity. This is achieved by designing systems that can parallelize work effectively, balance loads, and remain responsive even under heavy usage.

Real-World Analogy:
Imagine a busy call center. Each operator (goroutine) handles calls (tasks), and a central switchboard (channels) routes calls efficiently. The system scales as more operators are added, and the workload is distributed evenly.

2.4. Testing for Quality and Reliability

Testing is not an afterthought; it is an integral part of software development that ensures your system behaves as expected under all conditions.

- **Unit Testing:**
  Testing individual functions in isolation helps ensure that each piece of your system works correctly. Unit tests should cover both normal and edge cases.

- **Integration Testing:**
  Integration tests verify that the components of your system work together seamlessly. For an API, this means testing that HTTP endpoints produce the expected responses.

- **Table-Driven Tests:**

  This pattern allows you to define multiple test cases for a single function in a concise and organized manner, improving coverage and reducing duplication.

- **Test Automation:**

  Continuous integration (CI) systems run your tests automatically whenever changes are made, ensuring that regressions are caught early.

Real-World Analogy:

Think of testing as quality control in manufacturing. Every product is inspected at various stages to ensure that it meets standards before it reaches the customer. Similarly, comprehensive testing ensures that your codebase remains robust and reliable.

2.5. Integrating Multiple Concepts

A robust system seamlessly integrates modular design, error handling, concurrency, and testing. Each of these components reinforces the others:

- Modular design reduces coupling, making it easier to isolate errors.

- Robust error handling ensures that failures in one module do not cascade into the entire system.

- Concurrency allows your system to handle multiple requests efficiently while still providing clear points of failure for testing.

- Thorough testing verifies that each module behaves correctly under normal and exceptional conditions.

This integrated approach is essential for building scalable systems that remain maintainable over time. In our capstone project, you will see how these concepts come together to form a cohesive and robust architecture.

---

3. Tools and Setup

Before you begin coding, it is crucial to set up your development environment with the right tools and organize your project structure. In this section, we provide a detailed guide to configuring your tools for maximum productivity and scalability.

3.1. Required Software and Platforms

For this project, you will need:

- **Go Compiler and Runtime:** Obtain the latest version from the official Go website.

- **IDE or Code Editor:** Options include Visual Studio Code, GoLand, or Sublime Text with Go support.

- **Command-Line Interface:** Use Terminal (macOS/Linux) or Command Prompt/PowerShell (Windows).

- **Version Control System:** Git for tracking changes and collaborating with team members.

- **Testing Tools:** Utilize the built-in testing package and consider third-party libraries like Testify for advanced assertions.

- **Optional – Continuous Integration Tools:** Tools such as GitHub Actions or Travis CI to automate tests.

3.2. Configuring Your IDE

A well-configured IDE can significantly boost your productivity:

1. **Download and Install:**
   Download Visual Studio Code from code.visualstudio.com or your preferred editor.

2. **Install Go Extension:**
   Open the Extensions pane (Ctrl+Shift+X), search for "Go," and install the official extension.

3. **Enable Code Formatting and Linting:**
   Configure gofmt and golint in your settings to ensure a consistent coding style.

4. **Set Up Debugging:**
   Install and configure Delve (dlv) for stepping through your code and diagnosing issues.

5. **Create a Workspace:**
   Create a dedicated folder for your capstone project (e.g., go-robust-system) and open it in your IDE.

3.3. Command-Line Setup

Make sure your command-line environment is ready:

- **Verify Go Installation:**

  Run:

```bash

go version
```
to confirm that Go is installed.

- **Familiarize Yourself with Commands:**

  Learn commands like:

```bash

go run main.go
go build
go test -v ./...
```
- **Initialize a Go Module:**

  In your project folder:

```bash

go mod init github.com/yourusername/go-robust-system
```
This creates a go.mod file for dependency management.

3.4. Version Control and Directory Structure

Use Git to manage your code:

- **Initialize Git:**

  In your project directory, run:

```bash

```

```
git init
git add .
git commit -m "Initial commit: Capstone project
setup"
```

- **Recommended Directory Structure:**

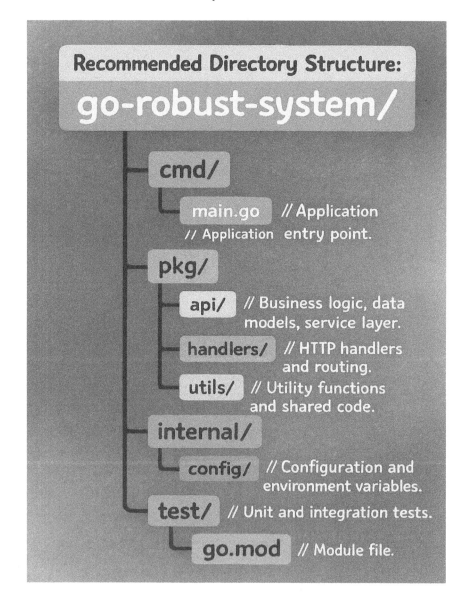

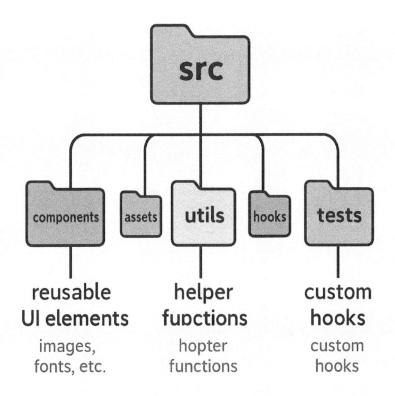

4. Hands-on Examples & Projects

In this section, we bring theory to life with practical examples and build a complete capstone project—a robust system that integrates topics from previous chapters. This project will simulate a real-world challenge and showcase how to design, implement, test, and optimize a full-featured system.

4.1. Project Overview

Our capstone project is to build a robust inventory management system for an online retailer. The system will:

- Expose a RESTful API with endpoints to create, read, update, and delete items.

- Handle errors gracefully and return meaningful responses.

- Integrate with an external database (for demonstration, we will simulate a database using in-memory storage).

- Support concurrent processing of requests.

- Include comprehensive tests for each endpoint.

4.2. Designing the Architecture

Before writing any code, it's important to plan the system architecture. Our system will be divided into several layers:

- **API Layer:** Exposes endpoints for CRUD operations.

- **Service Layer:** Contains business logic and manages data.

- **Data Access Layer:** Interacts with the simulated database (this could be replaced with a real database later).

- **Utility Modules:** Contain shared functions such as error handling and logging.

4.3. Implementing the Data Model and Service

We start by defining our data model and implementing the service that manages items.

File: /pkg/api/model.go

```go
package api

// Item represents a product in the inventory.
type Item struct {
    ID    int     `json:"id"`
    Name  string  `json:"name"`
    Stock int     `json:"stock"`
    Price float64 `json:"price"`
}
```

File: /pkg/api/service.go

```go
package api

import (
    "errors"
    "sync"
)

// Service provides business logic for managing
inventory items.
type Service struct {
    mu     sync.RWMutex
    items  map[int]Item
    nextID int
}

// NewService initializes a new Service instance.
func NewService() *Service {
```

```go
    return &Service{
        items:  make(map[int]Item),
        nextID: 1,
    }
}

// GetItems returns all items in the inventory.
func (s *Service) GetItems() []Item {
    s.mu.RLock()
    defer s.mu.RUnlock()
    result := make([]Item, 0, len(s.items))
    for _, item := range s.items {
        result = append(result, item)
    }
    return result
}

// AddItem creates a new inventory item.
func (s *Service) AddItem(name string, stock int,
price float64) Item {
    s.mu.Lock()
    defer s.mu.Unlock()
    item := Item{
        ID:     s.nextID,
        Name:   name,
        Stock:  stock,
        Price:  price,
    }
    s.items[s.nextID] = item
    s.nextID++
    return item
}

// UpdateItem modifies an existing item.
func (s *Service) UpdateItem(id int, name string,
stock int, price float64) (Item, error) {
    s.mu.Lock()
    defer s.mu.Unlock()
    item, exists := s.items[id]
    if !exists {
        return Item{}, errors.New("item not found")
    }
    item.Name = name
    item.Stock = stock
```

```go
    item.Price = price
    s.items[id] = item
    return item, nil
}

// DeleteItem removes an item by its ID.
func (s *Service) DeleteItem(id int) error {
    s.mu.Lock()
    defer s.mu.Unlock()
    if _, exists := s.items[id]; !exists {
        return errors.New("item not found")
    }
    delete(s.items, id)
    return nil
}
```
Explanation:

The service layer manages inventory items using a thread-safe map and a mutex. It provides methods for retrieving, adding, updating, and deleting items while handling errors where appropriate.

4.4. Building HTTP Handlers

Next, create HTTP handlers that interface with the service layer. Place these in the /pkg/handlers directory.

File: /pkg/handlers/handlers.go

```go
go

package handlers

import (
    "encoding/json"
    "net/http"
    "strconv"

    "github.com/yourusername/go-robust-system/pkg/api"
)
```

```go
// APIHandler handles HTTP requests for inventory
items.
type APIHandler struct {
    Service *api.Service
}

// NewAPIHandler returns a new APIHandler.
func NewAPIHandler(service *api.Service) *APIHandler
{
    return &APIHandler{Service: service}
}

// GetItemsHandler responds with a list of inventory
items.
func (h *APIHandler) GetItemsHandler(w
http.ResponseWriter, r *http.Request) {
    items := h.Service.GetItems()
    w.Header().Set("Content-Type",
"application/json")
    json.NewEncoder(w).Encode(items)
}

// AddItemHandler creates a new inventory item.
func (h *APIHandler) AddItemHandler(w
http.ResponseWriter, r *http.Request) {
    var input struct {
        Name   string  `json:"name"`
        Stock  int     `json:"stock"`
        Price  float64 `json:"price"`
    }
    if err := json.NewDecoder(r.Body).Decode(&input);
err != nil {
        http.Error(w, "Invalid input",
http.StatusBadRequest)
        return
    }
    item := h.Service.AddItem(input.Name,
input.Stock, input.Price)
    w.Header().Set("Content-Type",
"application/json")
    w.WriteHeader(http.StatusCreated)
    json.NewEncoder(w).Encode(item)
}
```

```go
// UpdateItemHandler updates an existing inventory
item.
func (h *APIHandler) UpdateItemHandler(w
http.ResponseWriter, r *http.Request) {
    idStr := r.URL.Query().Get("id")
    id, err := strconv.Atoi(idStr)
    if err != nil {
        http.Error(w, "Invalid ID",
http.StatusBadRequest)
        return
    }
    var input struct {
        Name   string  `json:"name"`
        Stock  int     `json:"stock"`
        Price  float64 `json:"price"`
    }
    if err := json.NewDecoder(r.Body).Decode(&input);
err != nil {
        http.Error(w, "Invalid input",
http.StatusBadRequest)
        return
    }
    updatedItem, err := h.Service.UpdateItem(id,
input.Name, input.Stock, input.Price)
    if err != nil {
        http.Error(w, err.Error(),
http.StatusNotFound)
        return
    }
    w.Header().Set("Content-Type",
"application/json")
    json.NewEncoder(w).Encode(updatedItem)
}

// DeleteItemHandler removes an inventory item.
func (h *APIHandler) DeleteItemHandler(w
http.ResponseWriter, r *http.Request) {
    idStr := r.URL.Query().Get("id")
    id, err := strconv.Atoi(idStr)
    if err != nil {
        http.Error(w, "Invalid ID",
http.StatusBadRequest)
        return
    }
```

```go
    if err := h.Service.DeleteItem(id); err != nil {
        http.Error(w, err.Error(),
http.StatusNotFound)
        return
    }
    w.WriteHeader(http.StatusNoContent)
}
```

Explanation:

These handlers process incoming HTTP requests, validate input, call the service layer methods, and handle errors by sending appropriate HTTP responses. They use JSON for both requests and responses.

4.5. Main Server Setup

Now, assemble the complete system in the main server file located in /cmd/main.go.

File: /cmd/main.go

```go
go

package main

import (
    "log"
    "net/http"

    "github.com/yourusername/go-robust-
system/pkg/api"
    "github.com/yourusername/go-robust-
system/pkg/handlers"
)

func main() {
    service := api.NewService()
    apiHandler := handlers.NewAPIHandler(service)

    http.HandleFunc("/items", func(w
http.ResponseWriter, r *http.Request) {
        switch r.Method {
```

```
    case http.MethodGet:
        apiHandler.GetItemsHandler(w, r)
    case http.MethodPost:
        apiHandler.AddItemHandler(w, r)
    case http.MethodPut:
        apiHandler.UpdateItemHandler(w, r)
    case http.MethodDelete:
        apiHandler.DeleteItemHandler(w, r)
    default:
        http.Error(w, "Method not allowed",
http.StatusMethodNotAllowed)
    }
})

log.Println("API server is running on port
8080...")
log.Fatal(http.ListenAndServe(":8080", nil))
}
```

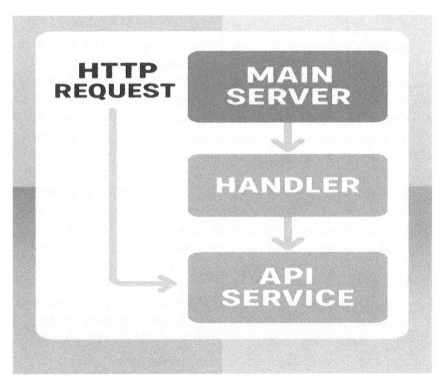

4.6. Testing the API

Testing is critical to ensure your system behaves as expected. Create tests in the /test directory to cover each endpoint.

Example Test: /test/api_test.go

```go
package api_test

import (
    "bytes"
    "encoding/json"
    "net/http"
    "net/http/httptest"
    "testing"

    "github.com/yourusername/go-robust-system/pkg/api"
    "github.com/yourusername/go-robust-system/pkg/handlers"
)

func TestAddItemHandler(t *testing.T) {
    service := api.NewService()
    handler := handlers.NewAPIHandler(service)

    payload := []byte(`{"name": "TestItem", "stock": 100, "price": 9.99}`)
    req, err := http.NewRequest("POST", "/items", bytes.NewBuffer(payload))
    if err != nil {
        t.Fatal(err)
    }
    rr := httptest.NewRecorder()
    handler.AddItemHandler(rr, req)

    if status := rr.Code; status != http.StatusCreated {
        t.Errorf("handler returned wrong status code: got %v want %v", status, http.StatusCreated)
```

```
    }

    var item api.Item
    if err := json.Unmarshal(rr.Body.Bytes(), &item);
err != nil {
        t.Fatal(err)
    }

    if item.Name != "TestItem" {
        t.Errorf("Expected item name 'TestItem', got
'%s'", item.Name)
    }
}
```
Explanation:

This test simulates a POST request to add an item and verifies that the API returns the correct status code and item details. Similar tests should be created for GET, PUT, and DELETE endpoints.

.

4.7. Running and Reviewing the System

Once you have implemented and tested the API:

- **Run the Server:**
  Use:

```bash
go run cmd/main.go
```
and access endpoints (e.g., http://localhost:8080/items) via a browser or Postman.

- **Review Logs and Output:**
  Check your console output for server logs and error messages.
  Make adjustments as needed.

- **Iterate on the Design:**

  Based on testing and feedback, refine your code structure, error handling, and API responses.

5 . Conclusion & Next Steps

In this capstone chapter, we integrated everything you've learned throughout the book to design, build, and test a robust system using Go. We began by discussing the importance of scalable design and modular architecture, then covered key concepts such as RESTful APIs, error handling, concurrency, and testing. By breaking down the monolithic approach and refactoring it into distinct, maintainable packages, you have learned how to create systems that are both resilient and scalable.

We walked through a complete project—a small API for managing inventory items—that demonstrated:

- **Modular design:** Splitting your code into packages like api, handlers, and utils for clear separation of concerns.

- **Robust error handling:** Propagating errors with context and returning meaningful HTTP responses.

- **Concurrency:** Using Go's built-in tools to handle multiple requests efficiently.

- **Testing:** Writing unit and integration tests to ensure the API behaves as expected under different scenarios.

- **Advanced optimization:** Employing strategies such as dependency injection, caching, and performance profiling.

These practices and techniques are essential for building systems that can grow and evolve without becoming unmanageable. As you move forward in your career, consider these next steps:

- **Extend Your System:**

  Add new features, such as user authentication, payment processing, or real-time notifications. Expand your API and refactor further to accommodate additional modules.

- **Integrate with Real Databases:**

  Replace the in-memory data store with a real database. Explore drivers and ORM tools that can help you manage persistent data.

- **Automate Testing and Deployment:**

  Set up a continuous integration pipeline to run tests automatically on every commit. Tools like GitHub Actions, Travis CI, or CircleCI can help maintain code quality.

- **Study Advanced Patterns:**

  Learn more about microservices architecture, service discovery, and API gateways to further scale your systems.

- **Engage with the Community:**

  Participate in online forums, contribute to open-source projects, and attend meetups or conferences to keep up with industry trends.

Reflect on the journey from writing simple Go programs to building a full-featured, modular API. The skills you've acquired in error handling, testing, and system design will empower you to tackle even more complex projects in the future. A well-organized codebase not only improves development speed but also sets the stage for innovation and long-term maintainability.

Thank you for working through this capstone project. As you continue your development journey, remember that the foundation of a robust system lies in clear design, rigorous testing, and continuous refinement. Embrace these principles and let them guide you in building systems that are efficient, scalable, and ready for the challenges of tomorrow.

May your code be modular, your systems robust, and your development process ever adaptive. Happy coding, and best of luck as you build the next generation of high-performance Go applications!

www.ingramcontent.com/pod-product-compliance
Lightning Source LLC
LaVergne TN
LVHW022335060326
832902LV00022B/4046